TIPS FOR THE
SAVVY
TRAVELER

TIPS FOR THE SAVVY TRAVELER

||||| **DEBORAH BURNS** |||||

A Storey Publishing Book

STOREY

Storey Communications, Inc.
Schoolhouse Road
Pownal, Vermont 05261

*The mission of Storey Communications is to serve our customers
by publishing practical information that encourages
personal independence in harmony with the environment.*

Edited by William Overstreet and Gwen W. Steege
Cover and text design by Mark Tomasi
Production assistance by Susan Bernier
Indexed by Word•a•bil•i•ty

Printed in the United States by R.R. Donnelley
10 9 8 7 6 5 4 3 2 1

Library of Congress Cataloging-in-Publication Data

Burns, Deborah.
    Tips for the savvy traveler / by Deborah Burns
        p.   cm.
    "A Storey Publishing Book"
    ISBN 0-88266-971-0 (pbk. : alk. paper)
    1. Travel.   I. Title.
G151.B868 1997
910'.2'02—dc21
                                   96-53199
                                       CIP

DEDICATION

To Tess, Sean, and Thomas;
and to my globetrotting grandmothers,
my original inspiration

⑊⑊⑊CONTENTS⑊⑊⑊

ⅢⅢ FOREWORD ⅢⅢ

My earliest memories are of travel. My Texan daddy would pile the four of us kids into an old Nash Rambler at our home in Texhoma, right smack on the Oklahoma border, and we'd set sail for Corpus Christi to visit relatives.

Daddy, an engineer and an efficiency expert, didn't believe in spending a lot of money on restaurants or motels, so when we'd leave on one of those 700-mile excursions, we might as well have been confined in a NASA capsule, embarking on a nonstop twenty-five-hour trip to outer space. He packed our underwear in our sneakers to save room, and he even built a bed in the back of the Rambler so Mother could sleep while we drove.

When we did have to stay overnight somewhere, it would be in a comfortable rooming house, rather than in a fancy hotel. Travelers have rediscovered that today, and the "bed and break-fast" business is booming. When Daddy agreed to a meal out, it would be at a cafeteria, rather than at a more expensive restaurant, and I still remember the taste of the homemade barbecued chicken and warm apple pie.

Mother served as the navigator, steward, and trip psychologist. She could make our voyages bearable, if not quite fun. She'd bring out little surprises as the journey progressed — Life Savers in Amarillo, a game of license plates in Lubbock, some soda pop in San Antonio — and while she'd never think of herself as a "savvy" traveler, I did and still do. On our trips, and during our frequent moves, Mother taught us all to be organized, patient, and prepared. She encouraged us to entertain ourselves, and to have a dime in our pocket and a friend or relative to call in every city.

When my husband John and I embarked on an eighteen-month living experience in Italy and France, I needed all of Mother's patience and savvy. On our first night in Bologna, a city of 400,000 off the tourist trail, I cried after seeing our substandard hotel room with no view but lots of Fiat 500 street noise and exhaust.

We went out to dinner at a nearby *trattoria,* and laboriously studied the Italian menu and seeming outrageous prices. We were overcharged for tough veal, nondescript pasta, and a strange, fruity wine, but we couldn't negotiate because of our language inadequacy. We paid and left. I cried again.

Things got better as I mastered a few phrases of Italian, got the conversion rates down cold, and moved out of that hotel. John, meanwhile, was meeting challenges of his own. After we found an *appartamento* in a modest neighborhood, I sent him down to get some vegetables for dinner. I wished him luck as he headed out, dictionary in hand, looking very American in his Bermuda shorts, white T-shirt, and sneakers. From the kitchen window I could see him, in front of the tiny *groceria* across the street, negotiating furiously. He appeared at the door a few minutes later with three gigantic brown paper bags in his arms and a sheepish grin on his face. "I was able to get two kilos of beans for only 100 lire!" he said proudly. We had beans for a while, and John worked on his conversions.

We learned the importance of keeping receipts when our landlady insisted that the wool Oriental rug we had proudly purchased at the Saturday morning flea market was hers!

We learned the way summer rentals work in Paris when the owner of a beautiful Montparnasse apartment told us it would cost $1,500. "For the summer!" I asked. "Yes, for the summer," she answered. We decided to take it, and she asked for the $4,500 in advance. "What $4,500?" I asked. "For the summer rental," she answered. I learned, painfully, what *par mois* ("by the month") meant.

Then there was the time in Singapore when, vexed by a head cold and a long day of travel, I went down for a steam bath and massage. As I relaxed in the steam bath, I heard an explosion of laughter coming from the female attendants. Into the steam bath with me stepped a male, three-hundred-pound, Sumo-type Singaporean, *au naturel!* I pulled my towel up firmly, smiled politely, and moved on.

From my own experiences I've learned that travel can't be totally predictable, and that's part of the fun. My friend Deborah Burns has gone to great lengths to uncover the tips, tricks, and suggestions that will help you avoid hassles, stay on top of your trip, and get help when you need it. The book has helped me, and I suspect it will help you, too.

I applaud her efforts, and I wish you enjoyable trips, "with the breeze at your back and the sun in your face."

Martha M. Storey

Martha Storey
Executive Vice President
Storey Communications, Inc.

ˡˡˡˡ ACKNOWLEDGMENTS ˡˡˡˡ

The author would like to thank the following people for their contributions: Constance Oxley, Cindy and Paul McFarland, Jack and Annie Archambault, Pam Art, Susan Auerbach, Janet Auster, Kingsley Barham, Sharon Bray, Caroline Burch, Jim Burns, Rain Burns, Stewart Burns, Angela Cardinali, Sarah May Clarkson, Beth Connolly, Riva Enteen, Judie Evrard, Susan Fuhr, Cyndi Garrison, Bernie Graney, Sheila and Jack Higgins, Jan Keep, Margaret F. Lally, Pamela Lappies, Deirdre Lynch, Meredith Maker, Jill Mason, Ellen McCauley McGarty, Catherine McHugh, Tom McHugh, Peter Meyers, Margot Page, Ellen Scott of the Hoosac Travel Agency, Mary Smith, Bob Spicer, Gwen Steege, Martha and John Storey, and Troy Travel.

The world of travel is constantly expanding. I've tried to be as thorough as possible in this book, but my knowledge is limited to my experiences and those of the people I've talked to. Part of the joy of travel is making discoveries and solving problems yourself! If you have any tips or suggestions that you feel are especially useful, please write me in care of the publisher. If we include them in the next edition of this book, I will give you credit.

SETTING A COURSE

*If you go only once around the room,
you are wiser than he who stands still.*

— **Estonian proverb**

You don't need a lot of money to travel well. Too much money can actually make your trip less interesting, especially when you're traveling in places like Mexico and Asia. Nor do you need to be young and carefree. Some of the happiest travelers I've ever seen were members of a senior group, the "Gadabouts," that I met on a ferry going up the British Columbia coast to Alaska.

The single most important ingredient of successful travel is a positive attitude — the confidence that you can handle any situation that comes up, and a cheerful self-reliance that helps you turn disappointments into benefits. (So maybe you didn't get as good a fare as the person sitting next to you on the plane. Next time you'll know. Maybe this summer *was* the worst weather Europe has had in 100 years — but it was something remarkable you shared with the locals.)

Many people feel that, despite years of schooling, they weren't truly educated until they traveled. Travel not only gives you insights into language, geography, history, and the arts, but it also deepens and broadens your understanding of your own life. It takes you out of the comfort and complacency of the familiar, feeds your senses and your intellect, heightens your understanding and compassion, and introduces good friends and memories. Even unfortunate travel episodes are not without their value — you're usually wiser for having gone through them!

For me, seeing how people live in India and South America made me look at my country differently. So did hearing the opinions that people in other countries held about the United States. As you travel, whether in this country or abroad, many things will come into perspective, including your life, your work, and your place in the world.

Some people find their best side emerges under the particular conditions of travel. You may love being in charge of your own destiny and having all the essentials of life in one suitcase. Or you may be apprehensive about your health, the security of your home, or possible crises en route.

I hope this book helps make your travel successful — free of problems and full of discovery. In the process of writing it, I found that certain ideas kept surfacing, and because these tips seem to me to be the most important, overall, for successful travel, I've listed them below for quick review. You'll find more suggestions about most of them in the pages that follow.

✓ Start making plans early. The earlier you can commit yourself to your travel plans, the more options you'll have and the better the deals will be. Be firm and decide early about transportation arrangements.

✓ Focus on just a few places instead of many. Even in Europe, where things are relatively close together, travel time eats up your precious vacation. Stay in one area and discover its many dimensions — people, history, museums, music, food, ancient monuments, and so on.

✓ Read as much as possible about the place you're visiting. Browse in your public library, read all available guidebooks, and explore background information (the Greek myths, for example, if you're going to the Aegean). Try to get a sense of the culture, the politics, and the religion. Get a map of your destination and become familiar with it ahead of time.

✓ Once you're on your way, get your nose out of the guidebook. Guidebooks are for studying ahead of time.

✓ Travel light.

✓ Ask for a discount or you won't get it.

✓ Stay alert. Read the fine print, listen to announcements, and hang onto your possessions.

✓ Don't try to do everything. Slow down. Build into your schedule time to relax, to play, to be spontaneous (especially if you're traveling with kids). This will let you respond when something terrific turns up — a new friend invites you to visit his country home in France, for example, or there's room for you on a chartered sailboat cruising the Hawaiian Islands. (This doesn't contradict the first tip, above. Be firm about your major transportation plans, but flexible once you arrive.)

✓ Be discreet — don't flaunt your money. Carry your valuables on your person, keep them in the hotel safe, or leave them at home.

✓ Walk. Nothing compares with it as the best way to see the world. Be sure to bring sturdy, comfortable walking shoes, well broken in.

✓ Get up and out early to see how the day begins — whether you're in Boston or Bangkok.

✓ Try to speak the language. Don't be embarrassed. Embarrassment can be the enemy of enjoyment!

✓ Wherever you go, visit people who live there.

✓ Follow through after your trip. If a service was particularly good or bad, let the supplier know. Communicate with the new friends you made.

And if these tips were to be distilled into the two most important, those two would be:

✓ Be prepared.

✓ Be brave.

ⅼⅼⅼ WHERE TO GO ⅼⅼⅼ

This is the easy part. You may take a trip for the sun or for the people you know there. You may want to see something spectacular or something exotic. You may be seeking adventure or peace and quiet.

Start planning when you first get the travel itch. Send away for brochures from state and national tourist offices (see Useful Addresses, page 217). Ask yourself what you and your companions most like to do — visit people? have adventures? go to the beach?

Check the Internet. You'll find an astonishing wealth of travel information there. Consult Yahoo or the Whole Internet Catalog for travelogues. The World Wide Web can also link you up with other travelers having similar interests. (Refer to Useful Addresses.)

Plan your trip so that everyone will have fun, including the kids, even if that means making a special detour for a child-centered activity. This may seem obvious, but it's amazing how many parents plan trips that are strenuous for children (too much driving, too many tour groups, too little exploration and discovery). Then they wonder why their children hate to travel. (See Chapter 18, "Traveling with Children.")

Decide how long your trip will be and how you'll travel. If you'll be flying, choose the cities you'll fly into and out of and begin scouting for good deals.

Start developing an itinerary based on your interests. Don't worry about what other people consider "must-sees." You don't have to visit the Eiffel Tower when you're in Paris; there may be other things you find much more meaningful. Make sure the places you want to see will be open when you're there. Learn what the weather's like. Find out whether you'll be traveling during the most crowded season.

ⅢⅢ TRAVEL AGENTS ⅢⅢ

Look around until you find a good travel agent. A professional can be a valuable resource, sharing experiences and expertise, helping you plan and book a vacation, finding big discounts and special deals, and giving you the latest information on everything from new resorts to possible air-port hang-ups — almost always at no cost to you. With persistence, you may find one of those very special travel agents who is a real artist, who loves the work and is good at it — canny, patient, and imaginative, with a good memory and good computer skills.

Travel agents receive a commission from suppliers with which they do business — airlines, hotels, cruise lines, railroads, vacation resorts. (Be aware, however, that some travel agents don't promote dis-count flights because discounters don't pay commissions.) Travel agents charge the consumer directly only for arranging a very complicated itin-erary or for handling a large tour group; in the latter case, part of the total expense will be a modest travel agent surcharge.

To tell if you've found a competent travel agent, assess the degree of interest and care taken with you as a customer. Did your agent conduct a "personal profile" to determine what your needs and desires are and what your situation and budget will allow? Did your agent ask intelli-gent questions? If you asked a question that couldn't be answered immediately, did your agent promise that an answer would be forth-coming? Most of all, if you felt that you were treated courteously and professionally, chances are you made a good choice. If you're happy with a travel agency, use it regularly and recommend it to your friends. That's a good way to ensure that the agent keeps treating you as a VIP.

You should never feel pressured by a travel agent. If you do, you're with the wrong person. Travel agents deal with all kinds of customers, and they'll usually be glad just to sit and give you some vacation ideas and prices.

Tell your travel agent you want the best deal possible. Your agent should take into account special low fares, unusual deals that will get you where you're going more cheaply (for instance, by accompanying a package tour as far as your destination).

Don't hesitate to ask questions. In addition to offering such standard services as developing itineraries, making reservations, and issuing tickets, your agent should be able to tell you what you may need in the way of immunizations, how to go about obtaining a passport or visa, how to get to the car rental agency once your flight lands, and whether you should buy trip insurance.

ⅲⅼ FINDING A TRAVELING PARTNER ⅲⅼ

If you don't enjoy traveling on your own, hook up with another single traveler. Or you may choose to travel with a partner to get better deals (half of a double room is usually cheaper than a single room).

Before deciding to travel with another person, however, you may want to find out the answers to certain questions (see box). Most important is to agree that you're financially independent of one another; be sure that your partner is responsible with money and won't turn to you for help. Next most important, be sure that each of you respects what the other wants to do. Try also to get a sense of your partner's personal habits — are they compatible with yours? — and how he or she reacts in a crisis. The answers to these questions may not be reasons not to travel with a person; they're simply useful to know in advance. Flexibility and amiability are most important.

Trips can be ruined when two people don't get along. The best of friends can turn into enemies in the close quarters and constant companionship of a shared trip. Your memory of the Louvre, for example, might be completely colored by the fact that your traveling partner was sulking. If you have good communication, however, problems are solvable. Naturally, troubles are more likely to surface during a long trip, rather than on a week-long excursion.

Things to Know about Traveling Partners

- How do they handle finances? Are they extravagant or irresponsible, or do they spend as little money as possible?

- Does one aspect of the trip particularly interest them — shopping, mountain climbing, visiting museums, eating well, getting a tan — and does that coincide with your expectations?

- How do they react in a crisis?

- Are their habits compatible with yours? Are they neat? Are they night owls or early risers? Are they punctual? Are you? (Will one of you always be pushing the other to catch that train?)

- How will you resolve problems? Will one of you assume leadership and make decisions, or will you decide things together?

- Are they timid, adventurous, daring, or foolhardy? (Will one of you always be holding back?)

- Do they meet people easily?

- Is one of you good at a particular task (navigating, speaking the language, bargaining), and do you want to divide up such responsibilities?

Schedule regular time apart as one way to avoid problems. One day a week, for example, go off alone after breakfast, and then rendezvous at dinner or later to share your experiences. This way you can each do what you really want — shop, go to a museum, or sit all day in a sidewalk cafe — without worrying about a less-enthusiastic partner. When you meet up with each other again, you'll have new insights to share and a new appreciation for each other.

Consider pooling some of your money. A successful way to manage finances when traveling in a group, especially in a car, is to pool your money in a "kitty." Each person contributes the same amount of money, and all expenses are paid from the kitty. When the fund gets low, it's replenished. At the end of the trip, what's left is split equally. You don't have to argue over bills or worry about each person's share of gas. Keep track of what you put in and when, to monitor your expenses.

╷╷╷ GUIDEBOOKS ╷╷╷

Bookstore shelves bulge with travel books. As idea books, they make for fascinating browsing and provide many useful tips, such as the hours a museum is open or the nearest subway stop to the Roman Forum. They are particularly useful for lodging information. But don't follow any guidebook too religiously, even an alternative or unconventional guidebook, when it comes to deciding how you can best enjoy yourself.

Don't bury yourself in a guidebook. Some travelers cling to their guidebooks, noticing only the things described by the author and rarely opening their eyes and looking for themselves. Some travelers can recite entire paragraphs of description from their books.

Steer clear of itineraries laid out for you in a guidebook. Develop your own itinerary, one that matches your interests. Remember that the greatest travel experiences happen when you discover things on your own.

╷╷╷ ECOTOURISM ╷╷╷

Ecotourism is one of the best new developments in travel. Companies that offer ecotravel are socially responsible organizations that make sure that their trips do not harm the environment or disrupt the local economy. For example, ecotourism firms will choose only those hotels that dispose of waste responsibly, hire and adequately pay local labor, and promote activities that preserve the local ecology.

An exciting aspect of ecotourism is that it's a way you as a traveler can actually make a positive difference in the world. When tourists want to see the intact rain forest, and spend money to do so, it strengthens the argument within the host country that the rain forest should be preserved. Moreover, ecotravel to a developing country actually fortifies that economy.

Making the Most of It

You have only two or three days to visit a country or a city, yet you want to get the flavor of the place. Or perhaps you're intentionally planning a stopover as part of a longer trip. For example, you and your family are going to Ireland, but you're planning a three-day stopover in London or New York on the way. Here are some tips:

■ *Especially when adjusting to a new time zone, a new climate, a new language, or new driving patterns, take it easy on the first day. Allow yourself plenty of time simply to soak up the sensations of the new place.*

■ *Don't overdo it, trying to cram everything into a short visit. Plan one important activity per day, and let the rest of the day be spontaneous. Make sure the central activity is something everyone in your party will enjoy. Even so, your most memorable experiences may occur during your unscheduled time.*

■ *Avoid, or allow plenty of time for, heavily touristed areas. For example, a visit to the Statue of Liberty and nearby Ellis Island can take most of a day, if you include the ferries, waiting in line (often for three hours), climbing to the top of the statue, looking at the view, descending, eating lunch, and fully exploring the fascinating restored immigration center on Ellis Island. All this cannot be accomplished in just two hours. If you have only two days in New York City, this excursion would take up one of them.*

■ *Save time for relaxed strolling, the best way to discover a city.*

■ *Consider getting out of the big city by renting a car and driving to a smaller city or town. Stay in an inn or a B&B. Explore the place, discover its history and special features, eat the local specialties. From London, for instance, you could drive to the beautiful city of Salisbury and spend time visiting pre-Roman ruins and modern pubs. Your impressions of England may be deeper than if you had stayed in busy London.*

||||| 2 |||||

ᕈED TᕈPE

Even the most intrepid world explorer still has to go through the necessary steps of obtaining a passport and, often, visas. These processes should be started several months before departure. If you'll be driving while abroad, apply for an International Driving Permit at the same time.

You should also be prepared to deal with unfamiliar procedures when you reach your destination. In some countries, even making a phone call or mailing a letter can challenge you.

||||| PᕈSSPOᕈTS |||||

Apply early. If you don't have a valid passport, apply for it at least three months early. You will have to apply in person. For information about where and how to apply for a passport locally, contact your local courthouse, town or county government, or post office. If you do have a passport, check to ensure that it won't expire until well after you plan to return home. If your passport will expire within two months of your return, apply for a renewal passport three months before your departure date. You can do this by mail or in person.

Know the procedures. United States passports are now valid for ten years. As of this printing, a brand new passport costs $55, plus a $10 processing fee levied by the local authority executing your application. After you've submitted your application and photographs, repeated an oath, and paid the fee, the local authority will send your application on to be processed.

Passport Photographs

Note that your passport photograph must meet strict requirements or the application will be rejected, costing you time. It's worthwhile to have a photograph specially taken by a professional photographer who knows how to shoot and process photos for passports. In particular, the size of the image must be no smaller than one inch, and no larger than one and three-eighths inches, from bottom of chin to top of head (including hair). Also, the paper must be capable of standing up to a temperature of 225°F when the photo is mounted. Most vending machine photographs are not acceptable.

You may apply in person. The State Department, which issues all United States passports, has thirteen Passport Agency Offices where you may apply in person. They are located in Boston, Chicago, Honolulu, Houston, Los Angeles, Miami, New Orleans, New York, Philadelphia, San Francisco, Seattle, Stamford (Connecticut), and Washington, D.C. Refer to Useful Addresses, page 217.

To apply for a passport, you need:

✓ Two identical, recent, two-inch-square photos of yourself, full face, with a white background (see box)

✓ A copy of your birth certificate bearing the seal of the issuing authority, *or* your naturalization certificate if you are a naturalized citizen

✓ One additional piece of identification (such as a driver's license)

Be aware of potential problems. If you ever applied for a foreign passport, or in any other way began the process of renouncing U.S. citizenship, you will have to explain that situation to passport officials. Allow extra time for this.

Renew your passport by mail, if possible. You may apply to the National Passport Center (see Useful Addresses) if all of the following are true:

✓ Your passport will soon expire

✓ Your passport was issued less than twelve years ago

✓ You were at least eighteen years old when your most recent passport was issued

✓ Your name is the same as on the previous passport or you have legally changed your name and can submit a marriage certificate or court order to that effect

Obtain an "Application for Passport by Mail" (Form DPS-82) from your post office, a travel agent, or a Passport Agency Office. Complete the form, and send it to the National Passport Center along with your present passport, two recent passport-sized photographs signed on the reverse (see box), and a check for $55, payable to "Passport Services."

Once you begin your trip, keep your passport *on your person* at all times. Do not carry it in your suitcase, leave it on the airplane seat, or give it to another person who doesn't have a good reason for having it. Best of all is to carry it in a zippered pocket inside your clothes. Money belts are good; some travelers even carry their passport in a shoe!

Register your passport at the United States embassy upon your arrival in a foreign country. This greatly expedites getting a replacement if your passport is lost or stolen.

To get a new passport overseas, go to the U.S. embassy. The procedure will go much more smoothly if you have with you a copy of your birth certificate or your previous passport, an additional piece of identification, such as a driver's license, and some extra passport-sized

Passport Pointers

- If you've changed your name, include with your application for renewal a copy of your marriage license or the certified court order verifying your name change. Otherwise, the passport will be issued in the same name as the original.

- Allow at least a month to get your new passport, and more time (three months is safest) if you're applying in the peak season, spring.

- Apply in person, at any of the Passport Agency offices listed under Useful Addresses, if time is short. That way you can avoid some delays and explain any problems to the passport agent.

- If passport officials know your departure date, they will try to get your passport to you on time. If your departure date is ten days away, send proof of the date (copy of itinerary or ticket) to the National Passport Center along with a $30 check or money order. Please note that express mail charges are not included in this rush-processing fee.

- In an emergency you can get a passport in one day. Apply in person with your ticket or a letter from a travel agent at a Passport Agency Office.

- A service that will obtain your passport for you (overnight, or in one day if you come into the office in New York City) is Passport Plus (see Useful Addresses). Although based in New York, it operates nationwide.

photographs. You'll have to pay the full price of $55 for a new one, or in some cases you may be issued a three-month temporary passport.

VISAS

Consult travel agents, airlines, consulates, or embassies about whether you need visas for the countries you'll be visiting. No European country, for example, requires American citizens to have visas. Other countries have different requirements, however, and many require foreign nationals to obtain, and show, visas before they can enter. (The United States requires visas for most foreign nationals.) A visa is simply an endorsement of your entry into another country, and the granting of one indicates that your papers and your intended purpose (travel, work, study) are acceptable to that government.

Applying is mostly a formality. You apply for a visa in much the same way you apply for a passport. For most Westerners, obtaining a visa is simply a bureaucratic formality, because the governments involved are confident that we'll return to our own countries.

Write directly to the embassies or consulates of the country or countries that you plan to visit for an application. Usually, you need a valid passport and a photograph, and you must pay a fee. Some countries require proof of vaccination, as well; others need to know your exact travel plans, how much money you plan to take with you, your address in the country, and how and when you'll be leaving. Frequently, you must also declare that you have no intention of seeking employment in the country.

Pay a visa service if time is short or you're unsure about all the application procedures. Your travel agent will have addresses for visa services, which can be particularly helpful in obtaining difficult visas for countries where Westerners rarely travel or where restrictions on the freedom of foreign visitors may exist.

Package tour operators often take care of visas. But you must double-check. It is your responsibility, ultimately.

Countries Where Travel Is Restricted

If you plan to visit a country where travel is restricted, ask your travel agent to help you obtain the correct documents. To visit Cuba, for example (for humanitarian reasons or professional research), you not only need a passport and visa, but you must also apply for a specific license from the United States Treasury Department's Office of Foreign Assets Control.

Documents You Should Take Abroad

- Passport and visas

- Copy of birth or naturalization certificate

- Yellow International Certificate of Vaccination (see Chapter 4, "Health")

- Driver's license and International Driver's Permit

- Travel insurance claim form

- Extra passport photos — at least half a dozen

- Membership cards for any organization you belong to, such as the American Association of Retired Persons or the International Youth Hostel Organization, or a student card

- Basic medical information, including blood type, any special problems you have, allergies, and your doctor's address

- Extra prescriptions

Find out if you need a visa to cross a border by train. If you'll be traveling on a train that makes scheduled stops in other countries, you may need visas whether or not you get off. An official will board the train at the last stop before the border and ask to see passports and visas of all passengers. Your travel agent can look at the scheduled stops on your itinerary and advise you on visa procedures.

ⅠⅠⅠ DRIVING ⅠⅠⅠ

Obtain an International Driver's Permit from your local automobile club if you plan to rent a car. (You must be eighteen or older.) The only Western European country where you need it is Spain; elsewhere, your regular state driving license is sufficient. Outside Western Europe, many countries require an international permit. Even when not required, it's a good thing to have when driving in a country where you don't speak the language. The license is valid for one year, requires two passport-sized photographs and a fee of $10, and is issued automatically if you present a valid state driver's license.

Keep your license and permit handy. When driving, always carry both your state license and your International Driver's Permit.

ⅲ TELEPHONES ⅲ

Two things we take for granted in the United States are our pure tap water and our telephone system. Although advanced telephone technology is quickly infiltrating the most remote areas of the world, the problems of foreign telephone systems — even in highly industrialized countries — may surprise you.

Become familiar with the pay phone in the country you're visiting, both for convenience and safety. Many countries now have their own calling cards to operate pay phones. You can buy these at the post office or, in some countries, in shops. They come in different denominations or calling units. When you're about to leave the country, give your card to a friend or use up your leftover calling units in a long phone call home.

Find out when to deposit coins. In some countries, pay phones don't accept money until the connection is made; if you put a coin in when you pick up the receiver, you lose it. Often, when your party answers a loud buzz comes on the line until you insert the correct coins.

Use a calling card. The best bet for an international call is to use a calling card, such as the ones offered by AT&T and its competitors. One of the best new developments for travelers, calling cards allow you to access a long-distance dialing service much more easily and economically, whether you're calling from a pay phone, a hotel, or a private phone. Ask your long-distance provider if it has an international calling card for the specific country you'll be visiting.

Call from an International Telephone and Telegraph Office, if you're in a place without advanced telephone technology. It's often located in the post office. Use your telephone credit card, if you have one. Give the number you wish to reach to the clerk, who will put through the call and assign you to a booth. You pay when you're finished.

Use the telephone book in a foreign country; many foreign telephone directories have a page in English that can give you the number to dial for a multilingual operator.

> **Taxiphones**
>
> In some countries there are public telephones known as "taxiphones," because they calculate the cost of your call based on how long you talk and at what distance you're calling. Such phones require tokens; be sure to have a good supply at hand.

׀׀׀ M A I L ׀׀׀

You can receive mail at most foreign post offices. "Poste Restante," or General Delivery, at the main post office of the city is always reliable for receiving mail. To pick up your mail you'll need to show your passport. Note that post offices often close for the midday meal in foreign countries, and that the Poste Restante window may have even shorter hours than the main window. The post office will keep a letter for thirty days before returning it to the sender.

Pick up your mail at American Express. If American Express has an office in the country you're visiting, that's an excellent place to receive mail (and meet your fellow travelers!), as long as you have American Express traveler's checks or an American Express credit card.

Keep an eye on what you mail. When mailing a letter in some Third World countries, be sure to take it to the post office and watch the clerk cancel the stamp. Uncanceled stamps can be stolen off letters, especially in places where the cost of one stamp can buy a full meal.

Write postcards to yourself. If you're not the type who buys souvenirs, this is a good way to have a postcard of a favorite place or monument, and some postage stamps, as a special remembrance upon your return. It's also a good way to use up extra change as you're about to leave a country.

MONEY

On a two-week trip to Switzerland, a friend watched with consternation as the dollar took a slow downward slide. Ten dollars bought her twelve Swiss francs when she arrived but only ten by the time she left. How can you protect yourself against this kind of exchange-rate erosion?

Plan for the worst. When budgeting for your trip, imagine the worst, moneywise — that the U.S. dollar suddenly starts losing value against all major foreign currencies. Prepare for things to cost even more than you expect. To be safe, allow for a 20 percent increase in costs. You'll be pleasantly surprised if the dollar gains, rather than declines, during your trip!

Use credit cards and ATMs (see "ATM Systems," page 21). They can significantly reduce money hassles overseas. But be careful: when it's easy to obtain money it's also easy to overspend!

Establish priorities for your budget. On some trips, my companions and I have made eating well a priority; we saved on lodgings but splurged on the local cuisine. (In the tropics, for example, you might choose to eat in more-expensive restaurants to be sure of adequate sanitation.) In other places, lodging was paramount — we wanted to be right on the beach, or downtown in a city. You may wish to focus on entertainment — you're in London and you're willing to save on meals and lodging in order to attend the theatre every night. Even if you can't splurge on anything on your trip, it's helpful to have set spending priorities.

Think in the local currency. If you'll be in only one or two foreign countries, try to think in the currency of the place, rather than, for example, constantly converting rupees to dollars. Not only will this save you time whenever you're making a purchase — especially when you're bargaining a price down! — but it'll also help you understand the country's economics a little better. A handful of rupees may be worth a fraction of a dollar, which seems very little to an American, but it may be the average day's wage in the country you're visiting.

Take with you about $50 in U.S. currency in small bills for last-minute emergencies and, upon your return, for getting home again.

Ⅷ CHANGING MONEY Ⅷ

Sometimes the exchange rate may actually dictate where you go. If Venezuela is giving a good rate on the dollar, you might decide to go there instead of to the Bahamas.

Try to obtain, in advance, the equivalent of $50 to $100 in the currency of your destination. You won't get a good rate of exchange, but you won't have to worry about finding a bank and coping with long lines immediately upon arrival. Order your foreign currency at least a month ahead of time through your bank (the yen, for instance, can be hard to buy in the United States).

Look for the best exchange rate. Local banks, ATMs, and American Express or Thomas Cook offices usually give the best exchange rates. Avoid changing money at your hotel or in shops; an exorbitant fee is usually added. You'll find exceptions, however, in different countries — rely on guidebooks or on other travelers for advice. In Brazil, for example, hotels can have the best exchange rate, while in Switzerland, train stations may be best. In some socialist countries the rate of exchange is set by the government, and so it's the same everywhere.

Be aware of the banking hours. Banks in other countries tend to have fewer hours than they do in the United States. Many banks close for an hour or two at noon. In some countries a "banking holiday" closes all banks for two weeks every August. Be sure to find out the bank schedules in the country you're visiting.

Learn how the exchange system works. The bank will post a sign listing the exchange rates for the day. Under "U.S. $" there will be two columns, one headed "Buy" and one headed "Sell." In England, it might say £0.67 under "Buy" and £0.70 under "Sell." You're concerned with the "Buy" column, because the bank is buying your dollars. In this case, you'd get £10 for $15. The "Sell" figure is always higher than the "Buy" figure.

Know the currency. Having obtained some foreign money, take a good look at it. Examine the coins and figure out how to tell them apart. Look at the bills. You want to be familiar enough with them so that you can be as quick as possible in your monetary transactions. Also keep in mind that travelers often end up with pockets or purses bulging with change, from constantly breaking large bills. And change does not usually convert back to U.S. currency.

Bring along a pocket calculator to figure the exchange rate if you'll be doing serious shopping. *But don't get hung up on your exchange rate.* It changes from day to day and is impossible to predict. You can ruin your trip by fretting about the better rate available around the corner from where you cashed your check. And so often the difference amounts to only a few cents, not worth worrying about.

Save the receipts of all the money you change. Many countries require that when you leave you show these receipts if you want to convert local currency back to dollars (to ensure that you aren't making money off the black market).

> **Be Versatile**
>
> The best way to carry money is a combination of three methods: traveler's checks, credit cards, and plenty of cash, securely carried in a money belt.

ⅠⅠ ATM SYSTEMS ⅠⅠ

Many banks now belong to large national and international ATM (automatic teller machine) systems that allow you to get cash at all hours of the day or night and have it deducted from your checking account or charged to your credit card. Ask about this service at your bank or call the toll-free customer service number on your credit card bill. The machine will offer you a choice of languages.

Features of ATM Service

✓ You may be charged a small fee for each transaction in which you request cash at an ATM machine.

✓ There is a dollar limit to how much you can withdraw daily using your ATM card.

✓ If you use your credit card to withdraw money in certain countries, you may need to use a PIN (personal indentification number) code. Call your credit card company's toll-free number to obtain this, or ask your bank at home.

✓ Bring both a Visa card and a MasterCard, since many ATMs use only one or the other. Bring other cards as desired.

✓ When you use your ATM card to obtain cash overseas, you receive the local currency, not dollars. Make sure you know exactly what you can afford: is it 700,000 lire or 7 million? And you will be billed according to the rate of exchange on the day the charge clears in the United States, not the rate in effect on the day of the transaction.

ⅢⅢ TRAVELER'S CHECKS ⅢⅢ

Having your money in traveler's checks is obviously safest. Another advantage is that traveler's checks often receive a better exchange rate than cash does. This is not always true, however; traveler's checks are expensive to cash in some countries, such as Portugal. In Portugal the ATM is a cheaper way to obtain cash — if you can find one.

Get your traveler's checks early. Don't wait until the day before departure to purchase traveler's checks! There might be a snowstorm or a holiday you didn't bank on. If the dollar is sinking as you're making your trip preparations, and you believe it will continue to do so, you may wish to purchase traveler's checks in the currency of your destination, to "fix" an exchange rate. This is always a gamble, however — the dollar may suddenly start rising again.

Decide what denominations you want. Some travelers like to purchase small-denomination traveler's checks so they won't be carrying around a lot of cash. Others prefer to buy denominations no smaller than $50, so that they're not constantly cashing checks. I happen to be in the latter group. Some exchange places charge a set service fee per transaction, which can make it expensive to keep exchanging small amounts of money.

Keep a record. Before leaving home, make a list of the numbers of all your traveler's checks, and add the city and date purchased (see the Safety Numbers List, page 208). Give a copy of this list to a friend or relative at home and take a copy along with you in a sealed envelope in your suitcase. Keep the record of your traveler's checks separate from the checks themselves. If you carry the checks in your purse or money belt, keep the record in your suitcase. It's much harder to be reimbursed without this record.

Update your record daily. Since your record is separate from your checks, you'll be unable to write down exactly when you cash each check. Instead, update your record every evening. You don't need to remember where you cashed your checks — the important thing is to list the numbers of those you cashed. That way you'll have an accurate record of those remaining uncashed, in case they're stolen. Keep the receipt from each transaction with the record.

Cashing Traveler's Checks

You'll need your passport in order to cash traveler's checks. At some American Express offices, your traveler's checks must be American Express.

Immediately report missing checks. If your traveler's checks are lost or stolen, contact the nearest branch office of the issuing company and report the loss. You may be reimbursed right away. Have your passport with you. If you don't know the numbers of the lost checks (those remaining uncashed on your list), telephone or wire your own bank (or wherever you purchased the checks) or the friend or relative with whom you left a copy of the list.

ⅢⅢ CREDIT CARDS ⅢⅢ

Credit cards are a tremendous convenience on a trip. Not only do they allow you to postpone payment for transportation, lodgings, purchases, and so forth, but many can now also help you obtain cash. If you use your credit card to shop, you'll have a receipt at the time of the transaction, a monthly statement, and a period of financial float before you must pay.

Beware of overspending. It's very easy to exceed your budget by overspending on credit cards. If you wish to monitor your expenses, it might be wise to limit credit card use to particular types of expenses, such as emergencies and travel accommodations (transportation, hotels, meals).

Watch the exchange rates. Any foreign purchase made with a credit card will be converted to dollars for billing purposes, and many times the credit card companies will make that conversion at an inflated rate of exchange. Remember, they bill you according to the rate of exchange effective on the day your charge clears in the United States, not on the day you made the purchase.

Credit card acceptance varies. Credit cards are often accepted at hotels and good restaurants. Aside from these two instances, acceptance can vary from country to country. Some shops won't take them because they have to pay the credit card company a percentage of their total sale.

Different cards offer different advantages. Visa is the most widely accepted and used credit card in the world. American Express, on the other hand, offers you the broadest range of travel services. (For example, using an American Express Card to buy plane, boat, or train tickets automatically insures you for a set amount of travel accident insurance and baggage insurance.) With MasterCard Gold you receive many travel, insurance, shopping, and emergency-cash services.

Protect your credit cards. Leave at home any that won't be useful. Carefully guard those you do take. Make a list of the account numbers and the company's emergency phone number (see the Safety Numbers List, page 208) before you leave home. Give a copy to a friend at home along with your itinerary and the list of your traveler's check numbers, and take a copy along with you.

Check, then keep, your charge slips. When you charge something, examine the charge slip carefully before you sign. This is a good habit to get into (I've learned the hard way). Keep your customer copy so that you can compare it to your final bill. Your credit card company will help if there's a discrepancy. If you've signed an erroneous charge slip, however, then you'll most likely have to pay the bill.

You can obtain cash abroad with most credit cards (including American Express, MasterCard Gold, Visa, and Diners Club International). Check with the company for information. American Express cardmembers can cash personal checks from $50 to $150 by showing their card at selected hotels and airline ticket counters. In an American Express travel agency you can cash a bigger check and get part in cash and most in traveler's checks. Holders of the Sears Discover card or Diners Club card can cash modest personal checks at any Sears store or Citibank branch office, respectively.

ᴵᴵᴵ TIPPING ᴵᴵᴵ

In most areas of the world, those who serve you expect to receive a gratuity, or tip. The practice of tipping varies from country to country and can add confusion to an already foreign situation. Whenever you offer someone a tip for service in a foreign country, keep the following points in mind:

✓ As a general rule, 15 percent of the net bill constitutes a reasonable tip for all kinds of service.

✓ Check to see if your bill already includes a tip ("Service Compris"). In this case, an additional tip is unnecessary.

✓ A chambermaid receives no tip for a one-night stay, five to ten dollars a week for a longer stay.

✓ Porters are tipped according to the number of bags they handle for you — usually fifty cents per bag.

✓ Bellhops should be tipped one dollar per bag for bringing your luggage to your room.

✓ Barbers and hairdressers are tipped 15 percent of the net bill, with a minimum of one dollar.

✓ A taxi driver should be tipped 15 percent of the fare, but no less than twenty-five cents.

✓ Airport skycaps should be tipped one dollar or more for a full baggage cart.

✓ In some countries, doormen and ushers are tipped; find out what local custom dictates. As a rule of thumb, don't tip a doorman who merely opens a door for you or calls a taxi that's waiting at a stand. Tip a doorman fifty cents or more if he helps you with your luggage or finds a taxi for you on the street. Ushers who show you to your seat at a sporting event can be tipped between fifty cents and one dollar.

✓ Wine stewards (or sommeliers) are usually tipped 15 percent of the wine bill.

✓ Tour guides and leaders and bus drivers should be tipped.

✓ Observe the local customs. Tipping is strongly discouraged in China, Russia, Samoa, Tahiti, and Tonga. It is not generally practiced in Scandinavia, Switzerland, the Netherlands, and parts of Asia and Southeast Asia, as well as in a few countries in southern Africa.

✓ If you received especially good service, be sure that you hand-deliver your tip. Too often, those who take and profit from your tip are not the people who have earned it.

✓ Don't allow yourself to be bullied into overtipping. If you go above 15 percent, you make it harder for the next tourist.

✓ Above all, use your instinct. If service is good, acknowledge it in your tip.

If you'd like to know more about tipping customs in foreign countries, write to the International Federation of Women's Travel Organizations (IFWTO) for a handy little pamphlet on tipping (refer to Useful Addresses, page 217).

ⅢⅠ BEGGARS ⅢⅠ

Being approached by beggars, whether they are a gang of adorable street urchins, a mother with a crying baby, or a paraplegic on a temple's steps, can be a wrenching experience, and a challenge to your heart and your conscience. This is one of those situations where there can be no hard and fast rule.

Remember, however, that you will be approached again and again in some countries, whether you give money or not. If you give some coins to a mother with a baby, you may help her out for one day, but she will be in need again tomorrow. And you could give all of your money to beggars and not solve a minuscule part of that country's problems.

Watch what the locals do. In general, I don't give money to beggars, but there are exceptions. It's helpful to realize that in many developing countries begging is not considered despicable, but just a fact of life. Local people routinely give money to beggars who throng near places of worship. And I certainly would reward someone who performed a service for me — such as carrying my bags or watching my car.

HEALTH

There's a joke that says the only thing you really need in order to enjoy travel is a strong stomach. I would add, "And some common sense." Certainly the most important priority in traveling is to stay healthy; one of the most miserable experiences imaginable is to get sick when you're far from home.

I've heard that of all international travelers one-third suffer from diarrhea on their trip, with the fraction rising to one-half for those going to certain countries with poor sanitation. So what do the others do right? Some people are blessed with a robust digestive system; others simply take great care to stay out of trouble. (See "Diarrhea," page 37.)

GETTING READY

Schedule an appointment with your doctor for about six weeks before your departure date. You will need:

✓ A basic physical exam, including routine blood tests, a review of your medical record, and any necessary booster shots (tetanus, polio, etc.)

✓ A schedule of immunizations

✓ An updating of any prescriptions you require — enough to last the trip

Have your physician write out the generic or scientific name of your prescription drugs so that foreign pharmacists won't be confused by brand names. Your physician may also prescribe other medicines, to protect you against overexposure to the sun, diarrhea, and motion sickness. (En route, keep essential drugs and prescriptions handy; never pack them in luggage you'll be checking.)

Consider carrying a medical history. Older travelers in particular may wish to ask their doctor to fill out a sheet on their medical background, including blood type, drug allergies, special conditions, and other pertinent information. Have the physician include his or her address.

Have a dental checkup, too. I once tried to explore Dublin while suffering from a toothache, and it was a most unhappy day. Have your teeth cleaned and examined for cavities (x-rayed, if necessary), and have your fillings checked for secure fit. Obtaining dental care in a foreign country is a risky business.

Don't forget eye care. Make sure you take along copies of your prescriptions for contact lenses and glasses as well.

Wear a Medic Alert bracelet if you have a medical condition that should be known about in an emergency (diabetes, epilepsy, heart condition, pregnancy). To obtain one, contact the Medic Alert Foundation (see Useful Addresses, page 217).

Confirm what immunizations you should get, if any. (Pregnant women should generally avoid vaccinations unless absolutely necessary.) If your physician doesn't know, contact the International Travelers' Hotline of the Centers for Disease Control in Atlanta. (Refer to Useful Addresses for the telephone numbers.) You may be able to get inoculations for free or at a reduced rate at a branch of the U.S. Public Health Department or at your local or county public health clinic.

Obtain an "International Certificate of Vaccination" (often referred to as your yellow card) at the passport or public health agency. Your inoculations should be recorded on the certificate. This is required before entering some countries, and you'll find it a valuable lifelong record. Keep it with your passport.

Know what diseases you may encounter. One you need not worry about is smallpox — it's been eradicated. Diseases you may still see include, but are by no means limited to, the following:

✓ *Yellow Fever.* At this writing, only yellow fever shots are mandatory before going to certain areas of the world. A number of countries require proof of vaccination before visas are issued or entry is permitted. Yellow fever certificates are good for ten years. You should get this vaccination if you're going to any affected country. However, children under one year of age should not be vaccinated against yellow fever.

✓ *Cholera.* The risk of cholera for American travelers is very low, and the vaccine is considered relatively ineffective. Generally, if you avoid unsafe food and water your chance of contracting cholera is extremely slight. In 1991 the World Health Organization announced that a cholera vaccination was no longer required by any country.

✓ *Typhoid.* If you'll be traveling to Central America, South America, or Asia, and especially if you'll be visiting remote rural areas, a typhoid vaccination is strongly recommended (but not required). Plan to get the first shot a month before departure. The vaccine is administered twice, four weeks apart, and is good for two years.

✓ *Hepatitis A.* A gamma globulin injection will help protect you against hepatitis A and should be given if you're going to areas with poor sanitation. Although generally effective for three to six months, it's most effective immediately after being administered. If you get a booster during your trip, make sure the hospital or clinic has excellent sanitary standards.

✓ *Hepatitis B.* If you'll be in frequent close contact with people, for example as a health worker, teacher, or missionary, it is recommended that you be vaccinated against hepatitis B.

✓ *Malaria.* There's no approved vaccine for malaria, as yet. The disease is carried by mosquitoes, and is present in more than a hundred countries, especially in the rural areas of Mexico, Central America, South America, Africa, the Middle East, Asia (including India and Southeast Asia), and Oceania. If you travel to any of these areas, you'll be at risk, and you should protect yourself. Your doctor will prescribe a weekly dose of antimalaria medication, usually chloroquine, starting a week before you enter malaria territory and ending four weeks after you return home. In areas where the malaria parasite is resistant to chloroquine, you'll need to take an additional medicine called Fansidar. Ask your doctor if you need this. (Either medication may cause serious side effects; your doctor will advise you about these.) Check with the Centers for Disease Control to learn what medicines are recommended for your destination.

✓ *Measles.* It's wise to make sure you're immune to this serious disease. If you were born before 1957, you're probably naturally immune through having contracted it in childhood.

✓ *Tetanus.* No matter where you're going, you should have the primary series (two shots, four weeks apart) if you were never vaccinated, and a booster shot every ten years.

✓ *Meningitis.* Call your state Department of Health to find out whether any areas you'll be visiting have current epidemics of bacterial or viral meningitis.

✓ *Polio.* There are still areas of the world (tropical regions and developing countries) where polio is a threat. Contact your state Department of Health.

Use caution in remote places. *If you stay on the beaten path, or if you're merely visiting a city on business, your chances of contracting a serious disease are much lower than they are for the traveler who likes to explore remote areas.*

ⅠⅠⅠ W A T E R ⅠⅠⅠ

Water, which we in North America take so much for granted, may be heavily contaminated by disease-causing organisms in other parts of the world. Generally, the water in Canada, Northern Europe, Australia, New

You are traveling to a country where malaria is prevalent. How can you protect yourself?

■ *Contact your physician to obtain a prescription for the anti-malarial drug recommended for your destination. Begin the medication a week to two weeks before you enter malaria country, and take it for four to six weeks after you leave.*

■ *Between dusk and dawn, wear long-sleeved shirts and long pants in light colors. Dark colors and perfumes attract mosquitoes.*

■ *Check that window and door screens in your room fit tight, with a small enough mesh to keep mosquitoes out.*

■ *Use mosquito nets over beds (especially recommended for children). The best kind is rectangular, not cone shaped (so as not to touch your skin and allow mosquites to bite through it), and made of stiff white cotton with a wide border that can be tucked securely under the mattress. The ideal mesh is twenty-six holes per square inch.*

■ *During the day, tie the net in a knot and let it hang from the ceiling. When you open it, check carefully for mosquitoes. Repair holes with tape or needle and thread.*

■ *Some travelers spray their bed net, bed, and other areas of the room with a pyrethrin insecticide, which will kill mosquitoes instantly. Just remember that insecticides must be used with care.*

■ *Symptoms of malaria include fever with chills and headache. Do not interpret this as the flu — demand immediate medical attention. Malaria can be cured if discovered early.*

Zealand, and the United States is of excellent quality — sometimes even famous for its purity. If the water where you are going is not known to be up to these standards, however, you should drink only the following:

✓ Water that has been boiled or treated (see below)

✓ Beverages made with boiled water, such as coffee and tea

✓ Bottled spring or carbonated water and canned or bottled soft drinks

✓ Beer and wine

Give your system time to adjust to the drinking water, even if you're traveling within the United States. When flying from the West Coast to the East Coast, for example, it's wise to drink no more than one glass of water the first day of your trip.

In major European cities, tap water is generally excellent. The exceptions may be Italy, Spain, Portugal, and Greece — although travelers' experiences vary. If in doubt, purchase one of the many different brands of bottled water and have it with you in your hotel room.

Boiling is the most reliable way to treat water. Let it boil vigorously for five minutes, then allow it to cool, covered, to room temperature. Do not add ice. If you're at a very high altitude, boil the water for ten minutes or chemically disinfect it after boiling.

To treat water chemically, use iodine or halazone tablets. (Chlorine is slightly less reliable than iodine.) Add five drops tincture of iodine per quart or liter of clear water, or ten drops per quart or liter if the water is cloudy or very cold. Before drinking treated water let it stand for thirty minutes. If the water is cloudy or very cold, let the water stand from sixty to ninety minutes. Iodine is available from pharmacies and sporting goods stores, as are halazone tablets. If you use halazone, follow the manufacturer's instructions. If the water is cloudy or very cold, double the number of tablets and the standing time.

Other tips on safe water practices:

✓ If you cannot boil your water, strain it through a clean cloth to remove sediment, and then treat it with iodine or halazone tablets.

✓ You may use an immersible heater coil (if the voltage is appropriate) to boil the water.

✓ If the water is contaminated, ice will be, too. Use ice made only from boiled water.

✓ If a container has held unsafe water, it will contaminate fresh water poured into it. Be sure to clean all containers thoroughly before using them.

✓ Boil or treat unsafe water before brushing your teeth with it.

✓ Do not drink bottled noncarbonated water where there is inadequate sanitation, even if it is advertised as mineral water.

✓ If the water tastes bad, add a pinch of salt.

✓ Even the moisture that condenses on the outside of a can or bottle may be contaminated. Wipe off any moisture that has accumulated where your mouth will touch the container. Better still, use a drinking straw.

Go slowly if you intend to drink tap water. If you'll be living in a major city in a foreign country, where the tap water is of good quality, you may be able to adjust to drinking it if you take your time. Treat the water even before brushing your teeth, at first. Then use untreated water for brushing teeth and notice your reaction — if you experience any diarrhea, continue treating all water. If you have no ill reactions, continue boiling drinking water for shorter and shorter periods. Eventually, you may be able to drink it straight from the tap.

▥ ᖴOOD ▥

Enjoying the native cuisine and the local delicacies can be one of the greatest pleasures of traveling. When in an area where sanitation is poor, however, be very selective about what you eat. There are exceptions to most of the following tips; use them only as guidelines. If you learn to know your own constitution, you'll know how well you can handle strange foods.

Eat well-cooked foods that are still hot. Avoid anything that has been cooked but has been standing awhile.

Use caution when buying food from street vendors. A common warning is to avoid street food. This is a good general rule, but consult other travelers you meet. You might not want to miss the fresh juice of Mexico, the delicious broiled beef at stalls along the streets of Bolivia, or the famous night market, with food stalls, in Penang, Malaysia. Some travelers believe that the spicier the food is, the safer it is. Again, know your own metabolism. If you tend not to have digestive problems, try some samples; otherwise, don't take a chance.

Boil milk before drinking it, if you're uncertain about its quality. In many countries milk is as good as or superior to that in the United States. These are the countries where the government regulates every stage of milk production — Great Britain, Ireland, Scandinavia, Germany, the Netherlands, Switzerland, and many more. In places where the milk is not of good quality, however, avoid ice cream and soft cheese as well.

Food to Avoid in the Tropics

- Raw fruits — unless they can be peeled and *you* do the peeling. Stick to fruits that have natural protection in their peels, such as oranges, pineapples, and bananas (bananas come in many varieties in the tropics and are a true delicacy).

- Raw vegetables — especially salads. Well-cooked vegetables are usually safe.

- Raw or rare meat or fish.

- Unpasteurized milk or milk products.

⑭ DIARRHEA ⑭

You can take precautions against diarrhea without lessening the pleasures of your trip. Don't even brush your teeth with untreated water where sanitation is poor. Wash your hands before eating and after using the toilet. Eat only well-cooked foods, or fruits and vegetables that you peel yourself. Learn to quench your thirst with tea, coffee, bottled soda, and bottled carbonated water.

Know your enemy: A bout of traveler's diarrhea comes on suddenly and is usually over in three or four days. Go to a doctor if it persists for more than five days, if you see blood in your stool, if you experience fever or chills, or if you become dehydrated. *(Do not take Enterovioform for diarrhea.)*

Replenishing Fluids

The World Health Organization has come up with the following formula to replenish fluids lost during diarrhea. Prepare two separate glasses of the following:

Glass 1
- 8 ounces water (boiled or carbonated)
- 1 tablespoon honey, corn syrup, or table sugar
- ¼ teaspoon table salt

Glass 2
- 8 ounces orange, lemon, or coconut juice or 8 ounces water if fruit juice is unavailable
- ¼ teaspoon baking soda

Drink alternately from each glass. Infants should continue to breastfeed or take plain (treated) water as desired while receiving these solutions.

If you can't obtain the above ingredients, drink liberally of a variety of safe liquids, including treated water, canned fruit juices, hot tea with sugar, and carbonated drinks. Or take two tablespoons honey and two tablespoons vinegar in a glass of warm water, to replace fluids and minerals lost.

✓ Remember to drink plenty of fluids to prevent dehydration — a dangerous complication of diarrhea, especially for children. Dehydration is marked by excessive thirst and weakness in adults, and by listlessness and dry mouth in infants. Children in particular must be encouraged to drink a lot of clear liquids, such as bottled carbonated water. Add a pinch of salt and a pinch of sugar. Colas are fine.

What Would You Do If...

You are simply, miserably sick with diarrhea.

Ride out the illness for a day or two in a clean hotel room that has a clean bathroom, either attached or easily accessible, with a lock on the door.

✓ If you use Lomotil, use it only for one or two days. It will stop the diarrhea, but it will also prevent you from getting rid of the germs.

✓ Avoid cow's milk until recovery.

✓ Cut down on coffee consumption.

✓ Reduce your intake of solids. Eat bland foods — soft-boiled eggs, rice, potatoes, macaroni, crackers, bread — until you recover. In India ask for a dish called kedgeree, famous for restoring the health.

✓ If your child becomes sick with diarrhea, be especially vigilant in administering fluids. Dehydration comes more quickly with children and is a very serious problem. Contact a doctor if your child with diarrhea becomes feverish or otherwise appears ill.

ᴵᴵᴵ CONSTIPATION ᴵᴵᴵ

Many travelers, especially older ones, complain of the opposite problem — constipation. Laxatives are not the best answer because the body quickly can become dependent on them.

Eat a healthful diet — the best way to avoid constipation. Make sure you get fiber from a variety of sources, such as bran cereals, fruits, vegetables, beans, and whole-grain breads.

Get plenty of exercise, which seems to have a laxative effect on the body. Walking is best, and will be good for your health generally. Activities that tone the muscles of the abdomen — bicycling, yoga, and swimming — are also beneficial.

ᴵᴵᴵᴵ ON THE ROAD ᴵᴵᴵᴵ

The leading hazard for travelers in a foreign country is automobile accidents, undoubtedly because of unfamiliarity with foreign traffic laws. (See also Chapter 9, "Getting Around.")

Familiarize yourself with international highway signs before you get behind the steering wheel in a strange country. See the illustrations on page 110.

Make sure to wear your seat belt — do not rent a car that does not have them.

Use infant car seats. If necessary, invest in the kind of car seat that can double as an infant's airplane seat. Some car rental agencies will supply infant car seats, but usually you must return them to the city of origin.

Don't underestimate the effects of jet lag. Flights to Europe from the United States often arrive in the early morning, and passengers stumble blearily off and pick up their rental cars. In Great Britain and Ireland, they suddenly have to cope with driving on the left side of the road. Try to avoid difficult driving situations (a long drive, morning rush hour) under these conditions.

You can often prevent car sickness. Make sure no one smokes in the car. Eat a hearty breakfast before the trip and eat light snacks on the road. Avoid alcohol, and do not drink tea on an empty stomach.

Carry a first-aid kit. If you're traveling in your own car, camper, or boat, the American Red Cross has designed the perfect first-aid kit for you. Resembling a compact vinyl, foam-padded pillow, it unzips to reveal clearly labeled pockets containing bandages and sterile wipes, a waterproof blanket, a triangular bandage, and scissors. The sale of this kit supports the Red Cross. Write for the American Red Cross Automobile First-Aid Kit (see Useful Addresses, page 217).

First-Aid Kit

A small first-aid kit could include the following:

- Bandages
- Analgesics (aspirin or acetaminophen)
- Thermometer
- Sunscreen
- Nasal decongestant
- Tweezers
- Fingernail clipper
- Foil-wrapped sterile wipes
- Antibiotic cream
- Multiple vitamins
- Foot cream or powder
- Scissors

Other useful items to take, depending on where and how you're traveling, could include:

- Insect repellent
- Oil of cloves for toothache
- Water purifier — iodine drops or halazone tablets
- Calamine lotion (for insect bites, poison ivy, and sunburn)
- Motion sickness pills

ᛁᛁᛁ PERSONAL HYGIENE ᛁᛁᛁ

When traveling outside the United States, you'll quickly discover that in most of the world the daily shower is an undreamt-of luxury. Water, and especially heated water, are simply not that plentiful.

Adapt to what you find — whether it's a waterfall to bathe in on a beach in Mexico or that marvelous French invention, the bidet. In the tropics, rainwater is saved and carefully portioned out, yet your hosts, anticipating your needs, may go without a cup of tea themselves so that you can wash your face. If you can learn to be satisfied with a daily sponge bath instead of a shower, you'll be most comfortable.

Try a foot bath. Bathing your feet at the end of a long day can be almost as restorative as a hot shower. Take along, for example, some Pickle's Foot Cream, available from Caswell-Massey (see Useful Addresses).

Carry with you any health aids you find indispensable. I always bring dental floss, which often greatly amuses my hosts. Women will find that tampons are often available only in big cities.

> **Sexually Transmitted Diseases**
>
> Men and women who intend to have romantic adventures while traveling should be certain to bring their own supply of condoms. Do not expect your partner to be prepared.

Iᴵᴵᴵᴵ INSECTS Iᴵᴵᴵᴵ

If you're traveling in the tropics, you'll certainly notice the insects — they seem to be three times as big as they are here. Malaria is only one of the diseases carried by insects. Following the recommended regime of malaria prophylaxis will probably protect you from that disease, but you may wish to take other precautions as well in tropical countries:

✓ Use mosquito netting over beds and infants' cribs.

✓ Use insect repellent.

✓ Use mosquito coils, which are available in other countries and are effective.

✓ Wear long sleeves and long pants, in light colors.

✓ Be sure to be protected at dusk, mosquitoes' favorite time.

Watch out for ticks. To extract a tick safely from the skin, cover it with olive oil, mineral oil, petroleum jelly, or nail polish, any of which will force it to withdraw its head to avoid suffocating. Pluck it out with tweezers and disinfect the area.

Treat stings promptly. The normal reaction to a bee sting is pain, swelling, and itching. Relieve these with calamine lotion, an ice pack, and an analgesic. Although bees and wasps don't carry diseases, a few people are extremely allergic to their stings. A severe reaction can lead to death if left untreated and therefore constitutes a medical emergency. Find medical assistance immediately. In the meantime, remove the stinger as quickly as possible.

ᛁᛁ **SUNBURN** ᛁᛁ

Remember that the tropical sun can inflict a wretched burn on tender, winter-pale skin. If you're in a hurry to get a tan, you may instead get the burn of your life, which can be temporarily crippling. Take these precautions:

✓ Restrict your first day's sun-bathing in the tropics to ten minutes, the second to fifteen, and the third to twenty.

✓ Use a good sunscreen, and reapply after swimming or showering.

✓ Wear a hat and long sleeves at other times.

Swimming

Well-chlorinated swimming pools and the ocean are your best bets. In this country, swimming in freshwater ponds and streams is also usually (but not always) safe. In many parts of the world, however, you can emerge with one of a number of skin, eye, ear, or intestinal infections.

✓ Stay out of the hottest sun, from noon to three o'clock.

✓ If you do get burned anyway, use calamine lotion, vinegar, or the gel of the aloe vera plant to soothe the skin.

✓ Drink fresh fruit juices, or water with a squeeze of fresh lemon or lime juice.

SKIING

If you're on a ski vacation, give yourself time to recover from jet lag and adjust to the altitude, especially if you're out of shape. Otherwise, your judgment and reflexes may not be up to par. I once sprained an ankle skiing in Montana's high country the morning after a grueling night flight.

Take it easy for the first few days — get a good night's sleep and take a break every few hours during the day.

Protect your skin and eyes. Dazzling sun on snow can cause a severe sunburn. Make sure you apply a good sunscreen and, if your skin is tender, zinc oxide on lips and nose. Always wear sunglasses.

IF YOU GET SICK OR HURT

If you need medical attention while abroad you can contact the American consulate or embassy (or the Canadian, British, Irish, or Australian consulate) to find the name of a reliable English-speaking physician. American hospitals, large government-run hospitals, and missionary clinics are likely to have good physicians. If you have a serious medical emergency, the Overseas Citizens' Emergency Center under the State Department (see Useful Addresses, page 217) may be able to help out. It will notify your relatives of your problems, help transmit funds to you, and expedite the sending of medical information back and forth.

Before leaving home, consider joining IAMAT, the International Association for Medical Assistance to Travelers. IAMAT compiles an annual list of doctors in 125 countries who speak English (or another second language), meet the organization's standards, and agree to charge a specified fee. Membership in the association is free, although contributions are welcome. This important organization also distributes world disease and climate charts and produces a portable mosquito net. If you're traveling to a developing country or the tropics, you certainly should join IAMAT.

In the United States, carry the phone number for Hoteldocs with you. Hoteldocs (see Useful Addresses) is a service that will send a doctor to a hotel room within forty minutes of your call, at any time of day. All doctors have been recruited through the American Medical Asssociation.

Find out how to get after-hours help. For example, if you need a prescription filled after hours in Europe, every pharmacy will have on its door a sign listing the name and address of the pharmacy that is open that night.

Beware of unfamiliar drugs. Overseas you may encounter certain drugs that you should be careful of. Aminopyrine, sold as an analgesic in Japan, is very unsafe for people of Anglo-Saxon descent. Enterovioform has serious side effects and is considered of questionable value in treating traveler's diarrhea.

English-Speaking Physicians

To obtain the IAMAT listing of English-speaking overseas physicians, see Useful Addresses, page 217.

Know the payment rules. Although many European countries will give you health care for free under their public health systems, some will charge a high fee before admitting you to a hospital. Emergency assistance plans (see below) will come through for you in this situation. Major hospitals in large cities or American-owned hospitals may accept credit cards for service.

ⓛⓛ **INSURANCE** ⓛⓛ

Check with your insurance company well in advance of your trip to make sure you'll be covered wherever you go. Some policies, including Medicare, have geographic restrictions. Other policies may not fully cover costs incurred outside the United States. In addition to any special insurance you've acquired for your trip, you should be certain that your normal medical and health insurance is current.

Carry your insurance card, your agent's telephone number and address, and your insurance company's telephone number.

Take along an insurance claim form so that it can be filled out by the physician who treats you. Some companies, such as Blue Cross and Blue Shield, will not reimburse you unless such a form has been properly filled out.

Investigate emergency assistance plans. A form of insurance that is especially useful for travelers is the emergency assistance plan, which will give you money on the spot to help you through an emergency. It may also have a twenty-four-hour operator you can call collect to get immediate help. Teams of multilingual emergency assistance professionals will help you deal with any crisis, from getting a prescription filled in the middle of the night to getting evacuated after an accident. They can help you find a physician, dentist, or medical facility; may wire you money for hospital admission; will pay your hospital and medical expenses up to $5,000 or more; will contact your own physician in order to monitor the care you're receiving; and will arrange for you to be moved to a different hospital or back home. (Refer to Useful Addresses for names of companies.)

Know what limits and exclusions apply. For example:

✓ Some policies limit coverage of accidents involving active sports, such as skiing or scuba diving, unless you pay an extra fee. If you're going on a European skiing vacation, you can purchase a Carte Neige (literally, "Snow Card"), available through French travel agencies, which will provide emergency assistance and evacuation if you have a skiing accident.

✓ Many policies have an age limit, usually seventy. If you're a Medicare patient and would like supplemental coverage for a trip out of the country, contact the American Association of Retired Persons (see Useful Addresses).

✓ Third-trimester pregnant women are often excluded from coverage.

✓ In countries to which the United States government discourages travel, you may not be covered. Contact the Overseas Citizens' Emergency Center (see Useful Addresses).

✓ Some insurance plans offer coverage for one year, not just for a single trip. Directed primarily at the business traveler, such plans usually require that you not be outside of the country for more than ninety days at a time.

WHAT TO TAKE

The wisest travel advice of all is to take half the clothes and twice the money. Packing light is the first law of carefree travel. Yet it can be difficult, when you're actually packing, to leave behind that special sweater, those dressy clothes, that extra jacket . . . "just in case." It's as if you want to take a little bit of home along with you for security. Before you know it, you've got an unbelievably heavy, bulging, unwieldy bag.

Once on your trip, the weight of your bag becomes much more of a concern to you than the actual items you've brought. Rushing to catch a train, walking an extra mile to your hotel because you couldn't find a bus, constantly counting your bags to make sure you have everything — these are just a few of the times you'll curse the extras and wish you had been more disciplined.

Pack light. Not only will you be less exhausted if you pack light, but you'll also be much more flexible, mobile, and spontaneous. I have a particularly fond memory of walking across a South Indian mountain range for a day instead of having to take a grueling three-day bus trip the long way around — an option possible only because my luggage was just a small rucksack. When traveling with another person, aim to go light enough so that each of you can carry all the luggage, if necessary. This will be helpful, for example, if you have to find seats on a crowded train. One of you can go ahead while the other follows with the bags.

Select clothes that can be adapted for safety. Before you depart, I recommend sewing inner pockets to your clothes and adding buttons, snaps, or hook-and-loop tape, such as Velcro, to existing pockets. Back pockets of pants are especially vulnerable to pickpockets. Loose bills and change are safer in your front pants pocket than in a handbag. Women may want to add pockets to clothes that lack them.

Buy *after* you arrive. Remember that you can purchase at your destination clothes that fit the climate and the ambience. The silks of Asia and the cottons of the tropics are lovely and inexpensive. You can have clothes made for you in Asia. Woolens, on the other hand, are great buys in Northern Europe, South America, Australia, and New Zealand. (Occasionally, though, items purchased abroad may become just souvenirs of your trip, rarely if ever worn again — the daring bikini from the French Riviera, or the Indian sari.)

What follows are some tips to help you streamline.

ⅼⅼⅼ **CLOTHING** ⅼⅼⅼ

✓ Don't buy a new wardrobe before you go. (Save that money for your trip!) It's very annoying to drag around clothes that you don't like after all. Take your favorite clothes — familiar, comfortable things that you know look good on you. Everything you wear will be new to the people you'll be seeing.

✓ The most important items in your luggage are your shoes. They should be sturdy, with nonslip soles, and well broken in ahead of time. Even your dress shoes should be familiar and comfortable. You never know when you might find yourself on a romantic moonlit stroll along the Seine — an experience that would be ruined by blisters or sore feet. Have a cobbler replace heels and insert arch supports, if necessary. Give shoes a treatment with mink oil or other waterproofer. Take along some lamb's wool or bandages to prevent blisters.

✓ Take plenty of cotton or wool socks if you expect to be doing a lot of walking.

✓ The only items worth purchasing just before you leave are undergarments and socks, which can be hard to obtain on a trip. (These will give the same psychological uplift as all new clothes would!)

✓ Don't pack an article you rarely wear, thinking you might be in the mood to wear it. It will surely stay at the bottom of your suitcase the entire trip.

✓ Do not take expensive clothes that require dry cleaning, unless you feel very confident that the service will be good. Take things you can wash yourself, either by hand or at a laundromat, or that you can entrust without too much concern to a launderer. In some Third World countries, even the cheapest hotel will have a laundry service that comes to your door and picks up and delivers your things. These services are inexpensive and generally reliable, and the clothes will return after quite an adventure — being pounded on river rocks, baked in the sun, and given a knife-edge pressing. (Cottons respond well to this treatment; delicate items and knits do not.) Make a list of every item sent out.

✓ Choose your clothes for their lightness and washability. You want things that will stay wrinkle free, wash easily, and take up a tiny amount of space.

✓ Choose your clothes around one main coordinating color. Make sure each of your pants or skirts can be worn with each of your shirts or blouses.

✓ Scarves, belts, and costume jewelry, which don't take up much room, can change the look of an outfit from day to day or from day to evening.

What Would You Do If...

You're contemplating a trip to Tokyo and Singapore in March, and you don't know what the weather and temperature will be. How do you pack?

The International Association for Medical Assistance to Travelers (IAMAT) produces, for a donation, a series of world climate charts that include recommended seasonal clothing. The "Far East" chart says that in March Tokyo's temperature ranges from 35° to 53°F and suggests that you wear wool suits and dresses and warm overcoats. That same month, Singapore experiences temperatures in the humid 80s, so for comfort you should wear lightweight cottons, sunglasses, and sunhats.

✓ You may notice that women in other countries dress up more than they do in the United States, especially for dinner in a restaurant. And in many developing countries, local people do not respond well to female travelers who wear seductive or revealing clothes. Experienced women travelers pack (or purchase) below-the-knee cotton skirts or dresses to show their respect for the country they're visiting. Dressing with dignity is the key in a foreign culture.

✓ Unless you're expecting to dine with royalty, leave your expensive jewelry at home — in the safe-deposit box! It will only be a worry on your trip.

✓ Multipocketed safari vests, of the type photojournalists and fishermen wear, are wonderful travel garments for both men and women. Make sure some of the pockets have zippers.

✓ If you'll be encountering different temperature extremes, plan to layer your clothes. A turtleneck-shirt-sweater-shell combination will be warm enough for most climates. The shirt alone will suit warmer weather, and the shell will be enough for a cool evening.

✓ Similarly, if you'll be hiking, plan to dress in layers. A turtleneck, flannel shirt, and nylon windbreaker will be just as effective, more versatile, and much less bulky than a sweater.

✓ If you're traveling in winter, determine where you'll be spending your time. If outdoors, you'll need a warm coat, but if you're attending a seminar or otherwise planning to be indoors most of the time, you might get by with a raincoat and a warm sweater.

✓ Light, loose-fitting clothing is best in warm climates.

✓ Men should take along a sport coat (except, perhaps, to South Asia and Southeast Asia), and wear it en route. A tie can be rolled up and stuck in a corner of the suitcase.

✓ Business travelers must take more clothes than recreational travelers, since they must make an immaculate impression. A spilled cup of coffee can ruin the deal and the trip if you don't have a complete change of clothing. See Chapter 20, "Traveling on Business."

✓ Things the streamlined traveler can do without: pajamas and nightgowns (a T-shirt will do), bathrobe (a raincoat will serve just fine), fancy clothes, expensive jewelry.

✓ If you're packing light for a long trip, remember that you can live for three months with the same amount of clothes as for a week. It's easy to rinse out shirts, socks, and undergarments in the sink.

Travel Extra Light

A super-streamlined technique for the traveler who carries only a rucksack or an airline bag: Wear your bulkiest outfit — the suit, heavy sweater, boots, and/or overcoat. In addition, take one more complete, coordinating set of clothes. These two outfits can be worn in four different combinations. Generally speaking, don't include dresses, which are less versatile than separates.

✓ The ideal raincoat is crushable, dark enough to never look dirty, and flattering at any time. A handy combination would be such a raincoat, which can be rolled into a ball and stuffed into your suitcase or carry-on, and a fleece or down vest or parka that can be stuffed into its own little bag.

✓ Take a hat. A beret is a favorite for cold weather, since it always looks good on men or women. For warm places, take a crushable hat with a shady brim or visor.

✓ The black rubber galoshes people used to wear over their shoes are perfect for traveling. They take up very little space in your luggage and will save you from the discomfort and health hazard of wet feet if you're caught in the rain (especially in a country like Ireland that's frequently rainy). Also useful are the transparent plastic boots that women can pull on over their shoes.

✓ Take along a cover-up if you'll be spending a lot of time at the beach or poolside.

ⅠⅢ OTHER ITEMS TO TAKE ⅠⅢ

✓ Suitcase technology has come a long way in recent years. Rolling bags are much more convenient than they used to be. Check the Useful Addresses, page 217, for names of suppliers.

✓ Pick up a city or country map of your destination before you go, and become familiar with it. Locate your hotel and circle it on the map.

✓ In many foreign countries you won't find special brands of toiletries you or your family prefer. Any toilet items you consider essential should be purchased in advance and brought along.

✓ Many experienced travelers take toilet paper with them on trips. Some countries, particularly in Asia, do not generally have toilet paper in public bathrooms.

✓ If you take a hair dryer or portable iron on a trip abroad, also take an adapter. Unless you're traveling on business, however, it's best to avoid these items. Have your hair cut before your trip in an easy-care style, and bring wrinkle-free clothes.

✓ A sewing kit can be handy. Include several large-eyed needles, thread that matches the colors of your clothes, extra buttons, and plenty of safety pins. A fingernail clipper can serve as scissors. In Europe you can buy a multicolored braid of thread — when you need a certain color, you just pluck it from the braid.

✓ Take a good Swiss Army or other folding knife that includes a paring blade, bottle opener, and corkscrew. Pack it in your suitcase, not in your carry-on, purse, or pocket, to avoid problems at airport security checkpoints.

✓ Take a good padlock for lockers at health spas or hostels.

✓ Take along a net bag. You'll find it useful for shopping, laundry, wet bathing suits, impromptu picnics, and presents you take home for friends at the end of your trip.

Take extra copies of your passport photo in case your passport gets lost or you wish to apply for a visa, an International Driver's Permit, a fishing license, or any special pass. You can always leave leftover copies with your new friends to remember you by.

✓ When traveling extra light, you may have to wear glasses instead of contact lenses. The paraphernalia involved with contact lenses takes up more room, and the lenses are at constant risk of getting lost, damaged, or soiled.

✓ Laundry supplies could include concentrated liquid soap in a small plastic bottle, a stretchable clothesline, six little clothespins, an inflatable hanger or two, a sink stopper, a little clothes brush — or simply a bar of Ivory soap and a piece of string.

✓ Many travelers take along their own towel and washcloth, since hotel towels can be too few and too small. Yours should be a light weave, in order to dry quickly. A damp towel can dry hanging from the handle of a suitcase or pack.

✓ Prell shampoo can wash not only your hair, but your body and clothes as well. Because it's concentrated, one tube will last your entire trip.

✓ I've carried a small pair of binoculars around the world and been glad to have it. It's useful in any number of ways, whether you're looking at distant elephants in Kenya, porpoises off the bow of your cruise ship, a bullfight in Spain, or a concert in Central Park. Make sure to have four lens covers and a hard case.

✓ A roll of plastic garbage bags (taken out of the box) has dozens of uses, including carrying trash, laundry, shoes, toilet articles, wet bathing suits, and spillables. You can also use plastic bags to group small things, such as socks and underwear, that are otherwise easily lost in a suitcase. Such bags are especially useful when you're traveling with kids.

✓ A small immersible hot-water heater can be a real boon. You'll enjoy being able to relax with a cup of tea or coffee in your hotel room. Be sure to bring a few tea bags or foil-wrapped packets of coffee, as well as the correct adapter.

✓ If you take any foreign-made items abroad, you may have to pay duty on them when you return unless you have proof of prior possession. An insurance policy, a receipt or bill of sale, or a jeweler's appraisal will be acceptable. You can register items with serial numbers, such as watches, cameras, and tape recorders, at the customs office nearest you or at international departure areas. Keep the certificate of registration to use on your next trip.

PACKING

Well before your trip, examine your luggage to be certain it will hold up. It should be sturdy and rugged. Make sure zippers and handles are in excellent condition. Check seams for signs of strain. Ideally, every item of luggage should have a shoulder strap — make sure the rings that hold it on are strong and secure.

Choose appropriate luggage. If you have a large suitcase and expect to be walking only at the airport, then a set of wheels on the suitcase makes sense. In other situations they can be awkward, cumbersome, and inconvenient (they don't go up stairs, over curbs, or onto buses easily). Take two small bags with shoulder straps, rather than one larger bag, if you think you'll have to carry your luggage a lot.

Couples traveling together should bring separate suitcases. Each partner should pack a few of the other's clothes, in case one of you loses your bag.

To repeat, pack light. Twenty pounds is plenty to carry. (Weigh your packed bag on a bathroom scale.) One way to pack light is to put out on your bed everything you absolutely have to take — and then put half of it back into your closet.

Perform a trial pack a week before you leave. Examine everything for loose buttons, rips, and sagging hems. Put everything, including toilet articles and other nonclothing items, in your suitcase, and walk around the house with it. If it's heavy now, it'll seem three times as heavy a few days into your trip. Streamline before you go, to avoid having to jettison cargo during your journey!

Protect yourself against spills. Put liquids (shampoo, cosmetics, etc.) in plastic screw-top containers, which can be obtained in pharmacies, and tape the tops closed. Place them in plastic bags. Bring an extra roll of tape or some rubber bands along. If you bring a cosmetic bag, make sure it's plastic lined.

Tape to the inside of each suitcase your name, address, and itinerary, including addresses, phone numbers, and dates. Also enclose a list of the contents. This will ensure that you don't leave anything behind when you're repacking. (You can reuse this list, refining it for each trip.) Leave a copy at home in case your bag gets lost and you have to identify its contents.

Items to Keep Nearby

The following items should never be packed in a suitcase that will travel in the baggage compartment:

- Traveler's checks
- Business documents
- Negotiable stocks and securities
- Medicines
- Expensive jewelry
- Musical instruments
- Eyeglasses
- Matches or cigarette lighters
- Camera and film

Label the outside of your suitcase as well. If you're concerned about alerting potential burglars to the fact that your home is empty, you may wish to use your office address. Or you can tape an index card on your suitcase with your name on the outside and your address on the inside.

Prioritize the contents. Put things you might need in a hurry on top of your suitcase or in your carry-on bag — bathing suit, warm sweater, flashlight, toilet kit, sleepwear, or raincoat.

Lock your luggage and keep the key in your pocket or handbag.

Use a fanny pack to carry passport, tickets, keys, and wallet. Money belts are better for items that you won't need to be constantly using, such as extra cash and traveler's checks.

Roll your clothes into neat cylinders to minimize wrinkles. This space-saving tip from backpackers works well in suitcases, since you end up with a lot of tight rolls that fit together well. Roll several items of clothing together to get the fewest wrinkles.

Packing Pointers

- To reduce wrinkling, put plastic garbage bags on the bottom of the suitcase and between different layers.

- Stuff socks into your shoes and put the shoes in a plastic or cloth bag.

- Roll up sweaters and undergarments and fit them into the corner of the suitcase.

- Fold shirts, pants, dresses, and skirts as little as possible, and as close to the seams as possible, with buttons buttoned and zippers zipped.

- Place the heaviest things on the bottom of your bag and the more wrinkle-prone items on top.

- When you pack and repack, put things in the same place each time so that you'll be able to extract specific items quickly when needed.

Mark your suitcase in some distinctive way — with colorful tape, for instance — so that others cannot confuse your bag with theirs. Many travelers recommend fastening a luggage strap around each suitcase, not only to make it stand out from other similar bags, but to discourage pilfering.

A carry-on bag usually makes sense, whether you're traveling by plane, train, bus, or car; it's a good place to keep small, fragile, valuable, and frequently needed items. Industrywide regulations specify that each passenger may take on board a plane one suitcase or one garment bag. A handbag is also permitted. In fact, many passengers disregard these rules and most airlines don't enforce them. Passengers come aboard with full-length mirrors, cellos, potted palms, microwave ovens, surfboards, and grandfather clocks! This laxness has arisen because airlines have such an excellent record for safety. In an emergency, however, this extra baggage can become a hazard. During turbulence, heavy items can fall from the overhead compartments and injure people below. Lots of objects underfoot can impede an efficient evacuation or fuel a fire.

Additional Carry-on Items

Other items you might include in your carry-on bag:

- Reading matter
- Small flashlight
- Extra glasses and/or contact lens supplies
- Lip balm and/or skin moisturizer
- Slipper socks
- Earplugs or eye shade, if desired
- Nasal decongestant
- Travel alarm clock, set to destination time

A carry-on bag must fit under your seat (twenty by sixteen by nine inches). If it's soft and filled only with clothing, it may go in the overhead compartment. I like to travel with just a carry-on bag because I love the lightness and efficiency, and I love not having to wait the extra half hour for my luggage to emerge from the aircraft. Others, however, like to be less encumbered with bags en route, and prefer to send as much as possible in the cargo hold.

You can also carry on baby essentials. Parents traveling with infants or toddlers are allowed to take a diaper-changing bag and a stroller. But the child and the stroller may be more than enough to deal with: try to combine the baby's necessities and yours in one carry-on bag.

Pack a day's needs in your carry-on bag. You should have the essentials of life for the first twenty-four hours of your trip, in case your checked suitcase does go astray. This would include toilet articles, medication, and a change of clothing, such as a clean T-shirt, socks, and underwear.

ᛁᛁᛁ TRAVELING IN COMFORT ᛁᛁᛁ

Many women travelers claim that a full-skirted traveling dress is most comfortable and shows fewest wrinkles. Knits are also ideal. One friend who flies to France every year wears a giant black T-shirt dress, belted, with sandals. She can curl up and sleep on the plane but still look chic and unwrinkled on her arrival. Many, if not most, people who travel in this country and to Europe wear jeans en route.

Remember to take a sweater or light jacket, even in summer; planes are usually quite cool.

Consider wearing a jogging suit when flying. It can be very comfortable en route. Just be sure, though, to have a change of clothing in your carry-on bag. Someone I know wore a hot-pink sweatsuit for her flight to a conference in Europe, and her luggage went astray. She attended each of her seminars in the same pink outfit, because she had nothing else to wear. (Matters were made worse because sweatsuit material dries very slowly. After washing her outfit one night, she tried to hurry things up by hanging it over a lamp. She succeeded in burning a hole in her only outfit!)

Don't neglect your skin. In the dry air of an airplane cabin, many travelers complain of dry skin. Instead of moisturizer, you can use suntan lotion on your face and hands.

A FINAL CHECK

Develop the habit of running through a mental checklist, as you leave your home, to remind yourself of exactly where essential items are. Passport, tickets, traveler's checks, credit cards, necessary addresses, itinerary . . . you'll want to be sure you did indeed pack these and did not leave them on the hall table.

LAST-MINUTE DETAILS

Prospective travelers tend to devote most of their time and energy to preparation for the actual trip and don't make provision for the security of their homes. Don't forget to keep your house safe while you're gone.

Many of the following tips will require the help and assistance of a friend, neighbor, or relative. It would also be helpful to have someone serve as your emergency contact person while you're gone; leave copies of your important information with this person, who will be ready to help if anything goes wrong.

Offer in exchange your services as a house cleaner or errand person when you get back. This may help you feel less like you're imposing if you ask someone to take in your mail and water your plants.

You may have to hire someone to live in, and look after, your home if free help isn't available.

Give a house key and a copy of your itinerary to whomever looks after your home and takes in your mail. Be sure you have with you this person's address and phone number.

The fewer people in your neighborhood who know you're gone, the better. No one but the person who's looking after your home needs to know.

The most obvious signs of your absence are the most crucial. In addition to having someone gather your mail every day, suspend all deliveries: newspapers, UPS, the cleaner. No need to go into detail about your trip and your plans — you can telephone when you return and ask that service be resumed.

Home Security Tips

Make your house appear occupied to prevent being the target of burglars. Go through the house carefully with the following in mind:

- Lock all doors and windows, especially those on the ground level and with access to a roof or patio.

- If you have sliding glass doors you may want to make them extra secure with a locking bar (available at most hardware stores). Be sure to close any curtains along the length of the glass doors.

- Close curtains in the back of the house to prevent someone from boldly peering through the windows.

- Put your lamps on automatic timers, if you have them; if not, leave on some commonly used lights in bedrooms and kitchen.

- Always leave at least one bathroom light on and close the door. A bathroom is one place that could be occupied day or night.

- Close doors between rooms. Someone looking in to find out if anyone is home will only be able to see one room at a time.

- Tune the radio to a twenty-four-hour talk-show station, and turn the volume up to a conversational level.

- Buy fake security system decals that say, for example, "This house is protected by Acme Alarm Systems." Apply the decals to your outside doors.

- Ask a neighbor or friend to park a car in your driveway overnight, on the weekends, and for as much of the day as possible. This is one of the very best things you can do.

You'll enjoy your trip more knowing that you've taken the time to make the house secure, and whether your neighbors know you're gone or not, *your* care will also keep *their* homes safe.

A clear indication of an empty and inviting house is a yard with grass four inches high or a driveway blanketed with a foot of snow. In warm weather arrange to have someone mow your lawn once a week for the length of your trip. Get a recommendation from a friend for someone who does yard work. Pay this person in advance. Even if you'll only be gone seven days, you may not want to come home to a yard that immediately needs attention. Extend your vacation a little by having your lawn cut on the day you're due back.

In the winter engage a dependable person who will plow or shovel snow while you're gone. This person may ask for a refundable deposit — a small price to pay for a house that looks occupied and well maintained. If there isn't any need for snow removal, you should get your money back.

Pay all current bills if you'll be gone for more than one billing period, or arrange to have someone make payment for you. This is especially important in the case of homeowner's and life insurance. Be sure to take care of these well before you leave.

Clear the refrigerator of all perishable foods, defrost the freezer (if necessary), and then turn it off or down, even if your trip will be short. Turn down the water heater and the heat or air-conditioning.

Empty the garbage, and run the disposal while you pack the car with your luggage, so that you won't return to a house full of bad odors.

Unplug small appliances, particularly the television, stereo, and any home computer equipment. Violent storms can bring down power lines and create a power surge that could start an electrical fire where such equipment is plugged in. An electrical fire could mean catastrophe if no one is in the house to alert the fire department immediately.

Make two lists of important numbers, including those of your passport and all the credit cards, traveler's checks, and tickets you plan to carry. Add the companies' emergency/theft phone numbers (see the Safety Numbers List, page 208). Put one list in a sealed envelope and leave it with a friend or relative or the person who's looking after your home. Take the other list with you in a sealed envelope and keep it apart from your documents. Canceling credit cards from a foreign or distant location could be nightmarish if you haven't taken this precaution.

‖7‖

GOING BY PLANE

By shopping around you can fly for much less than others on the very same flight. The best fares belong to two types of travelers — those decided enough to make firm plans very early, and those flexible enough to get up and go at the last minute. If you start planning early, you have the most options.

Airlines overbook their flights because they assume a certain number of people will cancel. If all of the people who made reservations do decide to fly, someone will be "bumped" from the flight. You must reconfirm your flight three days before departure and arrive at the departure gate on time — or you may be the victim. (See "Getting Bumped," page 87.)

Make your reservation and purchase your ticket well in advance, if possible. Some airlines will give you a considerable discount — simply for the advantage of having your seats confirmed and paid for. Ask your prospective airline if it offers such an option. For example, if you book a summer flight on Aer Lingus during the previous winter, you can receive the less-expensive spring fare. This is why it is valuable to commit yourself early to your major transportation to and from your destination (but stay flexible once you're there!). With some discounts, you don't need to purchase the ticket until fourteen days before departure.

You may also get a sizable discount if you're flexible enough to make plans at the last minute and take advantage of the "short-notice discounting" that frequently takes place with international flights and, more and more often, domestic air routes. If a tour or charter isn't sold out close to departure time, the company may be desperate to fill the empty slots. These seats cannot be advertised, because that would be unfair to those passengers who paid full fare.

Discount travel operators have come into existence to make those seats available to you at discounts of 15 to 60 percent. Most of these discount companies require a moderate annual membership fee that covers you and your family or a partner. For that cost you may have access to a hot line or a newsletter listing bargain departures. Some companies include insurance. (For a list of operators, refer to Useful Addresses, page 217.) This kind of arrangement is not for the person who wants to go to a certain place at a specific time; it is for people who do not have rigid vacation schedules — the traveler who wants to head "someplace warm" on a cruise sometime during the winter, or to take a charter flight to Europe sometime in July.

Further Information
See also Questions to Ask When Making Airplane Reservations, page 204.

Flying "open-jaws" means you fly into one city and fly home from another. This is the most economical way to travel if your itinerary takes you to several different countries. For example, you could fly into Belfast, travel through Europe, and fly home from Istanbul, rather than having to return to Belfast. Charter services don't work this way; you have to fly into and out of the same city.

Certain people should not fly at all. Women whose pregnancy has progressed beyond eight months or who are in danger of miscarriage should not travel by plane. People with serious health conditions (such as a recent heart attack or recent abdominal surgery) should consult their doctors regarding the safety of flying.

If, like many travelers, you're anxious about flight safety, it may be comforting to know how very rare fatal airplane accidents are. According to the National Institute of Aviation Research at Wichita State University, in the last decade the chance of being killed in a plane crash was only one in three million.

ⅢⅢ FINDING THE BEST FARE ⅢⅢ

Deregulation has been the air traveler's best friend. Fares remain lower now than they were in the late 1970s, when deregulation passed. It also means you have a multitude of choices, even when airfare wars aren't raging. Unfortunately, the average traveler isn't aware of the vast array of options, partly because the fares change too frequently to keep up with them, and partly because the airlines would naturally prefer to sell at their higher fares. Sometimes even the reservations agent doesn't know every deal the airline is offering.

There may be many different fares for the exact same seat in coach class. Each fare is identified by a different code letter — Q, L, V, B, Y — and each has specific rules. For example, the Q fare may require a thirty-day advance purchase, a stay that includes a Saturday night, and a 50 percent penalty if the trip is canceled, with Tuesday and Wednesday being the cheapest days to travel. A V fare may be purchased two days ahead but may be nonrefundable and require a Saturday-night stayover, with any day of the week but Friday and Sunday being cheapest.

The lower the fare, the more restrictions, is the guiding principle of air fares. This includes expensive penalties if you cancel the flight after a certain date before departure.

Trip Cancellation Insurance

Trip cancellation insurance protects you from financial loss if you must cancel the trip for a good reason (your own or a family member's illness, for example) or if the airline or tour company goes out of business or cannot provide its services. It also will help out if you have to cancel when your trip is under way. Costing about 5.5 percent of the amount you want covered, this is a reasonable choice for someone taking an expensive tour or leaving behind a relative in poor health. Many people, myself included, never purchase this, but think it's a good idea anyway.

Always ask the airline reservation clerk if the fare stated is the cheapest available — clerks are unlikely to offer or seek that information otherwise. Ask whether flying midweek or Saturday is cheaper, or if there is a special fare on another date that would make it worth your while to fly then.

Midweek and midday travel may not only be cheaper than weekend travel, but also much less stressful. Or you may discover that if you can stay over a Saturday night your fare will be greatly reduced. Ask your travel agent or the airline reservations clerk to investigate such possibilities.

Online services and the World Wide Web offer a myriad of travel information and links, from electronic auctions to timetables to comparisons of tour packages to travelogues. Travelocity (see Useful Addresses, page 217), for example, offers timetables and prices, tips and recommendations, last-minute deals, bulletin boards, even quizzes. Note, however, that online services will not always indicate the best deal available. Try several different travel lines to find the best rate.

Charter flights are much cheaper than regularly scheduled flights — they may make an otherwise unaffordable trip affordable. You become a member of a group that rents an entire plane or just a block of seats on a regularly scheduled plane. Charter flights do, however, have drawbacks: they are irregular (you have to be flexible regarding your departure date); they tend to be crowded; if the aircraft doesn't fill up, the flight might be canceled; and if you're the one who must cancel, you won't get your money back unless you've purchased cancellation insurance in advance.

Make sure the charter company you book with has an escrow account. Your money will stay in this account until your trip is completed. This will protect you if the charter company should "go under" between the time you pay for your ticket and when you complete your travel. Either ask the reservations agent or have your travel agent check in *Jax Fax,* a charter newsletter.

Courier Flights

You can fly at greatly reduced rates to cities all over the world if you become a runner for a courier service. In this system, you agree to travel on a certain date and to pay a portion of your fare. You must arrive at the airport several hours before departure, meet a representative from the service, and receive baggage checks and paperwork. Look in the yellow pages of a "gateway" city phonebook (San Francisco, New York, Seattle, Los Angeles, Philadelphia, etc.).

Drawbacks include the likelihood of not being able to take any luggage (except carry-ons) and having to be very flexible about when you go. With some services, you must return on a certain date in order to get the best rate. You must dress conservatively and act professionally. But for people who like to travel light, this can be an extraordinarily good deal.

One reputable courier service is IBC Pacific (see Useful Addresses), which seeks couriers to fly out of Los Angeles or San Francisco to seven destinations in Asia: Bangkok, Hong Kong, Manila, Seoul, Singapore, Taipei, and Tokyo. The round trip, with return flights in seven to ten days, costs the courier very little — about $500 for a ten-day round trip between San Francisco and Bangkok. Note that there is no flexibility about the return date.

You can join the International Association of Air Travel Couriers (see Useful Addresses) and receive daily online bulletins regarding available courier flights.

You can also try to get a last-minute seat on a charter flight for even less than the already discounted fare. This requires maximum flexibility on your part, but if that suits you, it would be your best possible deal. Call a few charter companies to find out.

Inquire about excursion rates to Europe, which are often your best buy but come laden with restrictions. For example, you might have to buy the round-trip ticket thirty days ahead of time and stay away a minimum of seven days and no more than sixty days. You'll be penalized for changes made before and during your trip.

Consolidators are brokers who buy blocks of airline tickets and sell them at a discount to individual travelers. These are often seats that would otherwise remain unsold, and you can save up to 50 percent. *Jax Fax* (see Useful Addresses) is a monthly newsletter that lists these seats; they are also listed in the *New York Times* or other major newspapers. One disadvantage to these tickets is that other airlines don't honor them — if the flight is canceled, you're stuck.

Ask if there are standby fares on your route. These are less common now than a few years back, but you can still find them on international flights during "low season." The fares are greatly reduced but, unfortunately, it's very difficult to predict whether or not the plane will have seats available. Standby fares are only for those who can be completely flexible.

Travel clubs offer large discounts on air travel, but you must take at least two trips a year to make the cost of membership pay off.

The airlines that give the best fares frequently change. Check the ads in the travel section of your local newspaper and a major paper, such as the *New York Times*. Surf the Internet. Look for the smaller, newer companies. And remember that these airlines use the same equipment and adhere to the same safety regulations as the bigger names do.

Do not ignore the national airlines of small countries — you may be pleasantly surprised. My most comfortable flight ever was on Singapore Airlines, one of the most luxurious yet reasonably priced airlines you can find. In fact, customer surveys have rated Singapore Airlines, followed by Swissair and Cathay Pacific, the best in the world in terms of comfort, service, food, and punctuality.

Look in your newspaper for promotional fares the airline might offer for a short time only, perhaps to introduce a new route.

Use secondary airports (Newark instead of Kennedy, Oakland instead of San Francisco, Manchester instead of Heathrow or Gatwick). You can usually obtain a better fare.

Find out if a transatlantic flight will allow you to fly to other European cities without extra charge.

Once overseas, you can often find excellent airfare deals between major cities. Check the travel sections of local newspapers.

ⅢⅠ **FREQUENT FLYERS** ⅢⅠ

As with all currency, frequent flyer points are worth less than they used to be. More miles are needed to claim a free trip, certain routes give you fewer points than they used to, and more restrictions apply. Get a credit card that allows you to rack up frequent flyer miles with all your charges. Charge your airline, hotel, and car rentals on it, being sure to use the companies that are affiliated with your airline. For example, if you have an American Airlines Visa card, try to book your travel with American Airlines, your hotel room with Marriott or Sheraton (five hundred points), and your car with Alamo (five hundred points). A friend who travels frequently has obtained six free trips this way. What's more, she's received 10 percent discounts at the partner hotels and rental agencies.

Take advantage of your frequent flyer points to upgrade to first class if you're flying to Europe. The footrest, wider seats, ear plugs, eye shield, and excellent meals will make your flight more comfortable and the start of your trip that much easier.

It is no longer easy to fly on someone else's frequent flyer points. Airlines are vigilant in confirming that the passenger's name matches the name on the photo ID.

ⅢⅠ **MAKING A RESERVATION** ⅢⅠ

Be certain that you book your flight in the same name as your photo identification or passport. New security measures require that passengers be detained if these names do not match. An example would be if a woman's passport listed her maiden name while her ticket had her traveling under her husband's last name.

Use the phone or the Internet, and remember that you have many options — you can contact several airlines directly yourself and you can simultaneously have a travel agent working for you.

Telephone at least three different airlines to find out differences in fares. (Call toll-free information, 800-555-1212, to obtain their toll-free numbers.) Calling in the early morning or late at night offers the best chance of getting through quickly and of working out the best deal with the agent.

Write everything down — the phone number, the name of the airline, the agent's name, the date and time you call, the flight numbers and times, and the price.

Make sure you know if your flight is nonstop or direct (it flies to your destination, but makes one or more stops along the way), or requires a change of planes (a connection).

Try to arrange connecting flights with the same airline. If you can't fly nonstop or direct, your travel agent or reservations clerk should allow for the time you will need between connecting flights. Although this doesn't ensure that the first arrival gate will be near the connecting flight (arrival and departure gates can be located as much as a mile apart), the airline will feel some responsibility if your first flight is late.

Airport Resources

Travel agents have maps of all major terminals in a book called the *North American Travel Planner,* which also indicates wheelchair accessibility of terminals. The *Official Airline Guide,* another tome on the travel agent's bookshelf, lists minimum connecting times.

Do not take a flight that connects with under forty-five minutes for you to disembark and find the new gate. If you have only half an hour to make the connection and your first flight is late, you may miss the second plane.

⑪ SEAT SELECTION ⑪

Get seat assignments and boarding passes as soon as possible, especially if you have special requirements — you're disabled, you're traveling with small children, or you're a business traveler who needs to get quickly off the plane.

With American Airlines, at this writing, you may receive your seat assignment as soon as you make your reservation — as much as eleven months ahead of your departure date. With United Airlines, if you have a frequent flyer account you may book your seats very early. With most airlines you can obtain your seat assignment thirty days in advance.

Consider sitting by the emergency exit, if you're traveling without children. It makes you feel most secure, and the seats usually have a bit more legroom. However, many airlines now require that people in those seats be able-bodied adults who can help others exit the aircraft in case of an emergency landing. If that doesn't sound like you, ask for a seat right behind or across from the emergency exit. If you're traveling as a family, you will not be assigned those seats, because your first responsibility will be for your children.

> **Considerate Seatmates**
>
> A survey discovered that strong perfumes and excessive chattiness were among the most unpopular traits for a travel seatmate to have.

The next most desirable (comfortable and accessible) seats are aisle seats toward the front and bulkhead seats. On those airlines that permit smoking on international flights, the smoking section is in the rear of the aircraft. If you don't smoke, note that the back of the nonsmoking section may be uncomfortably smoky. The front row or bulkhead seats have a lot of legroom, but they usually lack a place to store your carry-on luggage, which can be a nuisance.

Ask for seats with a view of the lavatory door, if you're traveling with children or if you or your companion will need easy access to the lavatory. You can then know when there is a line waiting.

Have your seat assignment and boarding pass before you reach the airport. This saves time and aggravation, especially when traveling at holiday time. Also, check your baggage at curbside. (Don't use the curbside check-in, however, if you arrive at the airport late.)

A couple I know always books an aisle seat and a window seat in a three-seat row. Because a lone middle seat is always the last to be sold, these friends nearly always manage to fly with the luxury of an extra seat, with more legroom, extra storage space, and an extra tray table. This is especially helpful if you're traveling with a baby. If that middle seat is sold, its owner will undoubtedly let you sit together, since the middle seat has neither accessibility nor view. Make sure to give this person the choice of the window or aisle seat.

ⅢⅠ BUYING YOUR TICKET ⅢⅠ

Air fares are subject to change without notice. Once you buy your ticket, the airline cannot make you pay more if fares increase. If the price of tickets in your letter class goes down, you're eligible for a refund. If the fare goes down in a different letter class, however, then you may or may not receive some money back.

Purchase your ticket with a credit card. You'll have more luck getting reimbursed if the flight is canceled. In addition, if you use an American Express card, you get free flight and baggage insurance.

Call about two weeks before departure to find out when you can pick up your ticket and boarding pass, if you've purchased your ticket through a travel agent. Restrictions may limit how early the agent can issue the latter.

When you pick up your ticket, examine it carefully. Check dates, times, flight numbers, connecting cities, and so on, for accuracy. Make sure you have a page for each leg of your journey. Become familiar with the ticket so that you know which part will be removed when.

Write down the ticket number and keep it in a safe place as soon as you have your ticket (see the Safety Numbers List, page 208). Having a record of your ticket number will make reimbursement much easier if your ticket gets lost.

Purchase trip cancellation insurance early, if you've reserved a discount flight. The airline will not reimburse you, except under extraordinary circumstances, if you cancel.

Find out if the airline will mail you the ticket directly, if you should buy the ticket at a travel agency, or if you must wait until you reach the airport to pick it up.

ᴧᴧ **THE LAST FEW DAYS** ᴧᴧ

Reconfirm your international flight seventy-two hours before departure (a charter company can cancel your reservation if you don't), and to be extra sure, re-reconfirm one more time twelve hours before departure.

Reconfirm a dometic flight the day before departure. Your travel agent may reconfirm for you, but make sure of this. If you've reconfirmed and you show up at the gate on time, you're unlikely to get bumped. Write down the name of the representative you speak with, as well as the date and time of your call, in case any mix-up occurs.

If you have a cold, flu, or allergies, the American Medical Association warns that you may develop painful ear and sinus problems after experiencing cabin air pressure changes. Seriously consider postponing or canceling your flight, and if that's impossible, use an oral decongestant an hour before landing or a nose spray or drops before and during descent.

If you're pregnant, check with your doctor before taking motion sickness pills.

Try to get plenty of sleep the night before your trip.

Call to find out if your flight is on time before leaving for the airport. Allow yourself plenty of extra time to get to the airport — twice the normal time during rush hour and on Friday evening.

If the weather is bad on the day you plan to depart, call the airport to find out if flights have been canceled or delayed. If flights are only being delayed, find out *exactly* when departure is planned.

On your way out the door call the hotel to confirm that a room is waiting for you. Even if you've paid for everything in advance by cash or credit card, take the time to check your room reservations. This is particularly important if you won't arrive at your hotel until after 6:00 P.M. A phone call will let the people at the hotel desk know when you plan to arrive and can ensure that your room will be saved.

ılıl AT THE AIRPORT ılıl

Follow the airline's instructions regarding when to arrive at the airport. Especially with an international flight, you need extra time — two hours for passing through the security check, which can be very slow during the holiday season, and for clearing customs. If you arrive a little early, relax and enjoy the airport's shops and facilities and the marvelous opportunities for people-watching.

Check updated information on when the flight will leave, as soon as you arrive at the airport. If you find a line at the ticket counter, telephone the airline either on a courtesy phone or on the airline's toll-free number. You can also check the TV monitors that note flight arrival and departure times.

If an international flight is seriously delayed, do not pass through security and passport control too soon, or you may be stuck in a departure lounge with many fellow passengers and few facilities.

If you are late, do not have your ticket yet, and need to check your baggage, go to the front of the line and calmly explain your situation to the person waiting there. (That person may be waiting for the same flight!) If he or she refuses to let you go ahead, appeal to the ticket agent or to the next person in line. If there is anyone else behind the counter, he or she may be able to ticket you. Be sure you have all necessary documents in your hand.

Airline personnel make numerous announcements before each departure. ("TWA Flight 326 nonstop to Hong Kong is ready for boarding," "Flight 326 is now boarding," "Last call for Flight 326," "Flight 326

Making the Most of It

Stopovers may be part of your trip, either by choice or because of disjointed transportation schedules. Suppose you arrive in a city at 10:15 A.M. and your connecting flight doesn't leave until 3:45 P.M. That's a long time to sit in an airport.

Think about how to use that time. Does the airport have an efficient bus or subway connection to downtown? As long as you don't run into morning or late-afternoon rush hour, you might be able to see a little of the city you're passing through. I don't, however, recommend that you try to catch a glimpse of very large cities, such as New York, Los Angeles, or Chicago, or others that are far from their airports.

Study a map and choose a specific destination — a park, a restaurant, a museum, or a historic district to ramble through for an hour. In Boston, for example, you could take a subway directly from Logan Airport to the Boston Public Garden (Arlington Station) and enjoy a ride on the famous swan boats.

Allow yourself a minimum of one hour travel time, each way, and plan to be back in the terminal one and a half to two hours before your connecting flight departs.

now departing. . ."). It's a sickening feeling to arrive at the ticket counter only to have the agent say, "Your flight's been called. You'd better run!" I've had many, many close calls, yet so far have always made my flight. The usual reasons people give for missing planes are that their connecting flight was late, they were caught in a huge holiday crush either on the road or at the airport — or they lingered too long in the duty-free shop! Most of these problems can be avoided with careful planning.

If your plane is late and you have to make a connecting flight, inform the ground personnel as soon as you land and ask them to telephone the connecting gate or airline. Airlines do make an effort to hold a flight for confirmed passengers, if they know they are on their way.

Every airport has facilities for handling medical emergencies, ranging from infirmaries to full-scale hospitals. Ask any member of the airport or airline staff.

Ask at an information desk where you can change or nurse your baby. The number of airports with facilities for parents traveling with children is increasing. Some airports, such as London's Heathrow, have actual nurseries with cribs, toys, and trained staff.

LUGGAGE

Only a tiny percentage of the luggage taken aboard airplanes gets lost or even misplaced, but because of the volume of bags involved this may nevertheless happen to you. The following pointers should increase the likelihood that your bags end up where you do, and should minimize the hassle if they don't. (See also "If Your Luggage Is Lost," page 89.)

Make a list of everything in each suitcase when you pack. If your suitcase goes astray, you may need to identify everything in it. And if it gets lost, you'll want a list of the contents in order to file a claim for compensation. Keep a copy inside each bag to serve as a checklist every time you repack. Leave another copy at home.

Other Tips to Increase Luggage Safety

- Do not carry valuables inside your checked luggage.

- Do not carry liquids, cigarette lighters, or matches in your checked luggage.

- Lock your luggage.

- If your luggage is of a common type, add something to make it easily identifiable — stickers with your initials, contrasting tape, or a safety strap, for example.

- Allow plenty of time for check-in.

- Remove all old tags and stickers from your bag, which can confuse luggage handlers and send your suitcase where you went on your last trip.

- As soon as you retrieve your bag from the baggage carousel, check the lock.

- Do not leave your bags visible in a parked car.

Place a label with your name and address inside each item of luggage. Add a copy of your itinerary, with dates and addresses, so that anyone finding your missing suitcase can easily track you down. Also label the outside of each bag. Use your office address, if you wish, instead of your home address, so that you won't alert possible burglars to your empty house.

Many experienced travelers strap their luggage so that it won't burst open if it's handled roughly. Be very careful, however, that the end of the strap doesn't dangle, or it could get sucked into a conveyor belt.

Be sure you see the agent tag each bag when you check your luggage. Make sure each item is checked through to your final destination, if possible (note that the airline abbreviation is correct), and that you have the matching baggage claim checks in your possession.

Do not throw away your claim check. In some airports you must have it in order to remove your suitcase from the baggage area.

Never leave your bags unattended — not just because they may be vulnerable to thieves, but also because airport security officials may remove unattended luggage to look for explosives.

Do not subscribe to the "last on, first off" philosophy regarding luggage. Statistics show that lost luggage was usually checked in at the last minute.

ⅢⅠ **S E C U R I T Y** ⅢⅠ

Security measures have become more extreme in recent years. They are vitally important in keeping your flight safe. If passengers cooperate, the procedures should be smooth and efficient.

Security officers ask to see your ticket and a photo ID, to be sure both show the same name. They will examine your carry-ons and handbags with, at a minimum, X-ray equipment. You will pass through a metal detector. Sometimes a jackknife in your pocket will set off the alarm, and for this reason you may want to pack it in your luggage.

Some countries are more vigilant than others. At some airports, passengers are personally searched for weapons by male or female security guards. They will search your baby's stroller. Sometimes your luggage is searched by hand before being placed on the aircraft.

If you don't have a film shield, remove your camera and film from your carry-on bag, which will be scanned by the X-ray equipment, and either carry it through the metal detector or hand it to the security guard. For convenience, keep your film in a zip-closure plastic bag or carry both camera and film in a padded bag that can easily be removed from your carry-on.

Do not make jokes about terrorism. Security personnel will not find them funny.

⣿ ON BOARD ⣿

Take a blanket and pillow from the overhead rack before sitting down. These tend to disappear once the flight is under way.

Before takeoff, fasten your seat belt snugly around your hips (not your stomach), and make sure you know how to remove it quickly. Experienced travelers keep the seat belt loosely fastened even when the "Fasten Seat Belts" sign is turned off.

Tips to Increase Comfort En Route

- Sit in an aisle seat toward the front of the aircraft.

- Do not wear tight clothing or shoes.

- Slip out of your shoes (your feet will swell during the flight) and put on some slipper socks.

- Elevate your feet on a carry-on bag or a briefcase stowed beneath the seat in front of you.

- Eat lightly.

- Drink plenty of nonalcoholic, noncaffeinated beverages. A glass of water every hour is good.

- Put a pillow behind the small of your back.

- Take an occasional stroll around the cabin.

- Bring a sweater or jacket — airplane cabins are usually cool.

- Use lip balm on lips, moisturizer (or suntan lotion) for skin, and eye drops or contact lens lubricant to combat the effects of cabin dryness.

- Bring a toilet kit so that you can freshen up in the rest room before landing.

- Bring along a cassette player and earphones (but not a radio, which may interfere with aircraft navigation systems).

When you fly with an infant or a toddler, the safest option is to buy the child a ticket and to take along a carseat that is adaptable to a plane. Otherwise, hold the child on your lap, outside of your seatbelt, during takeoff and landing.

Be prepared for emergencies, despite the relatively good safety record of airlines. Read the instructions regarding emergency procedures, emergency exits (note where they are, and count how many rows are between your seat and the nearest exit), and how to operate safety equipment. Listen to the flight attendant's brief explanation of safety procedures, even if you've heard it a hundred times before. Pay particular attention, if you'll be flying over water, to how you put on and inflate the life vest — passengers in an emergency often regret not having listened to these instructions.

If you're traveling with a child, note that you should put on your oxygen mask first, and then help the child put hers on.

The relatively low air pressure in your aircraft can cause discomfort. Cabin pressure is equivalent to that at eight thousand feet above sea level. If your ears bother you during takeoff and landing (caused when the middle ear is affected by changes in air cabin pressure), try yawning, chewing gum, or doing this: pinch your nostrils shut, inhale, close your mouth, and try gently to blow your nose.

People with varicose veins should stroll down the aisle of the aircraft periodically, in addition to hoisting their feet up.

The air in the cabin will be very dry. Accept all of the flight attendants' offers of free beverages — choose plain noncarbonated water or fruit juices instead of caffeinated or alcoholic drinks, which will tend to dehydrate you. Bring a small tube of moisturizer or suntan lotion in your carry-on bag, along with some lip balm and some eye drops or contact lens lubricant. If your eyes begin to smart, remove your contact lenses and wear glasses. Unscented air moisturizers are available in aerosol form. Use one periodically to spray your face and the air in front of your face for a refreshing pick-me-up.

Exercises En Route

The following exercises, which can be done in your seat with your seat belt loosely fastened, are recommended by American Airlines. They stimulate circulation and stretch and relax cramped muscles. Try them with kids. They're especially valuable on a transoceanic flight.

- Lean your head as far forward as possible, feeling the stretch down the back of your neck. Lean your head to the side, keeping face front, and feel the stretch down the side of the neck. Lean to the other side.

- Let your head drop back, with jaw relaxed, and gaze at the overhead compartment of the row behind yours. Arch your upper back.

- Hug yourself, placing your right hand on your left shoulder and your left hand on your right shoulder. Lean your head forward and pull your shoulders forward.

- Roll your shoulders forward simultaneously, and then roll them back, arching your back. Then roll them in circles, first one and then the other, toward the front and then toward the back.

- Grab the back of your left armrest with your right hand and twist your upper body around so that you can look behind you. Do the same with the other side.

- Press your elbows down onto your armrests as hard as you can.

- Reach up toward your light with one arm and then the other.

- Loosen your seat belt and then lean over to the floor, stretching your arms as far as possible. Sit up slowly.

- Tighten the muscles in your buttocks and then release.

- Lift one foot off the floor by raising your thigh about an inch from the seat. Rotate your foot in one direction and then in the other. Repeat with the other foot.

If you're not crazy about airline food, take a tip offered by my well-traveled mother. She orders the vegetarian meal, which she has found to be much more attractive and delicious — perhaps because it's specially made — than the regular meals served to her seatmates. Other alternative menus include kosher, diabetic, low-salt, low-calorie, low-fat, high-protein, bland, Muslim, and Hindu meals. With any of these, you must order in advance. The airline does not carry special meals otherwise.

Avoid alcohol. Airline regulations stipulate that the only alcohol consumed aboard the aircraft must be served by your flight attendants. They will not serve any passenger who appears intoxicated.

International flights often offer a chance to purchase duty-free gifts. Liquor is generally more expensive, however, than in the United States. Know your prices ahead of time so that you can tell if you're getting a good deal!

When traveling alone, stay alert. A friend once paid no attention to an announcement that her plane was arriving in Cleveland. Bound for Pittsburgh, she hadn't realized that her flight included a stop. Believing she was at her destination, she got off the plane. Only after fifteen minutes in the airport did she realize she was in the wrong city. Luckily, she was able to reboard her plane and continue on to Pittsburgh. Most airports look the same, after all, so it's important to know the exact details of your flight.

Sleep Tricks

A sleep-inducing trick that never fails me: Close your eyes and rest your head comfortably against the wall or the edge of the seat. Relax your body. Now imagine that a great, soft broom is slowly sweeping your thoughts out of your head. As each new thought appears, the broom sweeps it away. The broom slowly clears away all your thoughts, and finally it sweeps away consciousness itself. You'll most likely be asleep. If not, try again.

Do not leave your purse, billfold, passport, or other valuables on your seat when you get up to stroll around. You should have your passport on your person at all times.

Experienced travelers make sleep a priority, especially on international flights. If you fly at night, bring along ear plugs and/or an eye mask. As son as the aircraft takes off, try to find an empty block of three seats where you can stretch out. You'll need every minute of sleep you can get if you're flying all night and arriving in the morning.

Purchase a neck pillow. This hooks around your neck and gives your head restful support.

ⅼⅼⅼ FEAR OF FLYING ⅼⅼⅼ

An estimated twenty-five million Americans, including someone as tough as boxer Muhammad Ali, share a fear of flying. For some, it's the height that brings on the dizziness and panic; for others, the loss of control; for still others, a fear of engine failure or the sensation of being confined. I've been plagued with this fear myself, and yet have managed to fly anyway.

Most who share a phobia about flying are afraid only during takeoff, turbulence, and landing. (It's difficult to be nervous during the tedium of a smooth flight.) One way to cope with your fear is to understand precisely what an airplane is doing throughout the flight — for example, when it makes strange noises.

Remember, every aircraft can take off, fly, and land safely even if an engine fails, and the pilots are prepared to deal with this.

If you can see the wings you'll notice elaborate adjustments being made to their shape by movement of the flaps during takeoff and landing. These changes increase uplift during takeoff and aid landing later. The passenger hears these movements and the rushing sound caused by increased air resistance. Just after takeoff you'll also hear the wheels being retracted, which sounds like the crashing of heavy doors.

The aircraft will probably bank just after takeoff, as it goes into a curve. Inside the cabin things may feel level, but you'll see the earth out one side of the aircraft and the sky out the other.

Some strong vertical air movements may jostle the plane, even though "air pockets" don't exist. The passenger will feel the jolt. The aircraft is designed to have the elasticity it needs and has been put through the severest of tests.

The descent on a long-distance flight begins more than a hundred miles before reaching the destination. An air traffic controller is deciding where in the sequence of inbound and outbound flights your aircraft will come. Planes are separated by three miles horizontally and a thousand feet vertically.

If the airport is very busy, the air traffic controller will put your incoming jet into a holding pattern, an area up to twenty miles from the airport where planes can circle around a radio beacon at different levels. The controller will guide each craft, a thousand feet at a time, down the various "floors" of the hold (there may be five floors at a busy airport).

The wing flaps assume their landing configuration about five miles from the airport. They move in degrees during landings, and the wheels are lowered. You'll hear a rumbling sound as the wheels lock into place.

Sometimes a pilot makes a rough landing on purpose, if the runway is rainy. Immediately after touchdown you'll hear a very loud noise as the pilot reverses the engine thrust, to help brake the plane. You may cheer — you made it!

Knowledge may be the best antidote to the fear of flying. Bring along a portable atlas so that you can look out the window and roughly follow the airplane's route over land. If it's clear, you may become absorbed in the landscape despite your fear. If it's not clear, look at the clouds and determine what type they are.

Tips to Help You Control Your Fear

- Arrive at the airport in plenty of time, to minimize stress.

- Sit toward the front of the aircraft, where the ride will be smoother and quieter.

- Sit in an aisle seat, so that your attention will be directed toward the activity in the center of the aircraft, not to the great space outside the window.

- Bring along a good book — a thrilling page-turner, if possible. For me, this is the most successful strategy.

- Relax as fully as you can. Imagine being in a serene place.

- If you're still afraid, confide in your neighbor or tell the flight attendant. It may help simply to feel less alone.

JET LAG

Jet lag is a state of extreme fatigue and disorientation caused by crossing multiple time zones with such speed that your body cannot adjust to the new schedule. (You don't suffer jet lag after flying north or south, only after flying east or west.) It's as if your body were trying to catch up with itself in the time it would've taken you to get there by land.

The condition is characterized by headaches, constipation, insomnia, nervousness, irritability, sluggishness, and forgetfulness, most of which seem to be symptoms typical of sleep deprivation. One famous U.S. diplomat blamed what he considered the major misjudgment of his career on fatigue caused by jet lag.

Some people seem to be immune to jet lag; others can be laid low for more than a week. Babies and children can adapt relatively fast, while older travelers report that they suffer more from jet lag as the years go by.

Jet lag after flying east seems to last longer and to be more difficult to cope with than jet lag after flying west, perhaps because it's harder for the body to adapt to skipping a few hours than to adding them on. Here are a few other tips to help you cope:

✓ Never schedule an important meeting within twenty-four hours of your arrival if you'll be flying across three or more time zones. Try to plan your trip so that you have a day to begin adjusting, or you'll be at a disadvantage during your meeting.

✓ Plan to arrive at your destination at bedtime.

Anti-Jet Lag Diet

One expert on jet lag is Dr. Charles F. Ehret, of the Argonne National Laboratory in Argonne, Illinois. He recommends a careful regime, starting a few days before your flight, that will help minimize the effects of jet lag.

A few days before your departure date, begin to alter your body rhythms in preparation for the new time zone. You can reset your body's clock by carefully rearranging eating and sleeping patterns. It's not as hard as it sounds.

If you'll be flying east on a transatlantic or transcontinental flight, three days before your departure have a "feast day," eating heartily of a high-protein breakfast and lunch, followed by a high-carbohydrate supper. At the same time, stop drinking tea and coffee. Two days before you leave, have a "fast day," eating the same type of meal but keeping portions small. One day before your trip, have another "feast day." On departure day, get up early, eat lightly during the day, drink a lot of water, and have several cups of strong coffee or tea at 6:00 P.M. Get a good night's sleep.

If you're headed west, do the opposite — start three days before with a "fast" day, alternate feast and fast days, and then eat well on your departure date. People I know say this diet does work, especially to relieve the digestive problems that typically accompany the beginning of a trip.

✓ Get plenty of sleep the night before your departure and the first night of your trip.

✓ The day before your departure, adjust your meal schedule to coincide with your destination.

✓ Sleep, if at all possible, during your journey.

✓ Avoid alcohol and caffeine on your flight.

✓ Dehydration can intensify the problems of jet lag. Try to drink at least one noncaffeinated, nonalcoholic beverage every hour while you're on the plane.

GETTING BUMPED

Getting bumped is not as common as you may fear. According to statistics from the Department of Transportation, fewer than five passengers are bumped for every ten thousand who fly. Holidays are when you're most likely to be bumped.

Overbooking is legal because so many passengers don't show up for the reservations they've made. If the airlines were required to hold these seats, they'd lose a tremendous amount of money. With the aid of computers, the airline counts how many no-shows have occurred on each flight, and based on this number it estimates how many seats to overbook.

If the airplane is full, the carrier is required to seek volunteers who will give up their seats in exchange for compensation. If an insufficient number of passengers volunteer, the airline will "bump" those still waiting at the gate. So to avoid getting bumped, check in early and board the plane promptly.

If the airline can put you on another flight that arrives within an hour of your original flight, then it need not pay you any compensation. If you'll arrive up to two hours later than originally scheduled, the carrier must pay you, to a certain limit, the cost of your ticket. If you arrive more than two hours late, the carrier will pay double the cost of your ticket, within a certain limit.

Sometimes instead of cash you'll be offered a free ticket. If you prefer cash, you can insist upon it.

In order to receive compensation, you must hold a confirmed and reconfirmed reservation, and you must have checked in by the airline's deadline. (Ask what this is — it can vary from ten to thirty minutes before departure for domestic flights, and more for international flights.)

You're not entitled to compensation if you didn't follow the rules regarding reconfirming and checking in or if you get bumped from a commuter plane (fewer than sixty seats) or from a plane flying to the United States from a foreign country. Usually, in the latter case, you'll be compensated to half the cost of your airline ticket, at the company's discretion — some foreign carriers won't reimburse you at all.

Some airlines promise not to bump a full-fare passenger. Check with your travel agent.

Even if you've reconfirmed and arrived at the airport on time, you must arrive *at the gate* by the time the airline has set or you may be bumped.

If you have a flexible schedule, you may not mind giving up your seat, arriving a few hours later than scheduled, and receiving compensation. Department of Transportation rules now require that airlines solicit volunteers before bumping passengers.

Before accepting compensation, find out the time of the next flight on which you can have a confirmed seat.

Make sure compensation will be enough to cover your expenses if the airline offers cash as compensation — hotel and meals, for example, if you have to wait for a morning flight. If the airline offers free tickets instead of cash, find out what restrictions these tickets carry. You may be able to negotiate your compensation.

The airline is required to give you the check or tickets immediately. Once you've accepted them, you will have a hard time demanding more later, so you must make a quick and accurate analysis of your needs.

ɪɪɪ CANCELLATIONS AND DELAYS ɪɪɪ

If your flight is canceled, the airline will usually arrange passage for you on the next flight out to your destination. Some discount airlines, however, may make you wait for their own next flight.

Most airlines no longer routinely provide hotel rooms, meals, and free phone calls to passengers facing long delays or cancellations. Now these services are offered only if the flight is diverted to an unscheduled location.

If your flight is seriously delayed, you may be able to insist that the airline clerk get you a seat on another airline. Before committing yourself to this second flight, however, make sure that it really will fly and that your original carrier will pick up any fare increase. If there is a long line at the ticket counter, you may find it easier to check with other airlines yourself.

ɪɪɪ IF YOUR LUGGAGE IS LOST ɪɪɪ

If your suitcase does not turn up, file a formal claim with the airline immediately, before leaving the airport — even though you have a week to do so. You may have to list the lost items, including their date of purchase and cost. Keep your claim form, baggage check, and ticket until you get reimbursed. It may take six months.

The liability limit for lost, damaged, or delayed baggage, as of 1997, is $1,250 per passenger, on all domestic flights on large aircraft (or on smaller aircraft included on the same ticket with large aircraft). On international flights, the Warsaw Convention limits liability to just $9.07 per pound of luggage. If the company estimates that your loss was less than this, it may pay you much less, or even nothing.

You can purchase excess valuation coverage to increase the airline's liability. This tends, in my opinion, to be too expensive (as much as $2 for every $100 of extra coverage). Baggage insurance available at airport insurance counters may be a better deal, covering your bags not just while they're at the airport but throughout your entire trip. Your own home-owner's insurance may also be adequate.

The airline will not accept liability for damage to fragile items, unless, possibly, they're still packed in the original factory-sealed carton, or are in special padded cases. Be sure you carry such items as musical instruments on board with you, or insure them separately.

If your bag is delayed, the airline may reimburse you for moderate out-of-pocket expenses to cover, for example, toilet articles and essential items of clothing. This payment will be small, at least initially, because the airline anticipates (and usually succeeds in) reuniting you and your bag in a day or two.

If Your Ticket Is Lost

If you lose your ticket, fill out a lost-ticket application. This is much easier if you jotted down the ticket number; otherwise you'll have to trace the number through your travel agent. Since the ticket is good for one year, you won't be reimbursed within that time.

If your bags get lost when you're far from home, the airline may pay you more money than if it were to happen on a homeward-bound flight.

If you check in at least fifteen minutes before departure time but your bag doesn't get on your flight, the airline usually assumes responsibility for delivering it to you when it finally arrives. If you check in less than fifteen minutes before your flight, it may not. Some will not even check baggage that late.

If your bag doesn't show up within three days, its chances of being recovered diminish markedly. Most airlines will search for it for about thirty days.

ⅼⅼⅼ HIJACKING ⅼⅼⅼ

Nonstop wide-bodied aircraft are statistically less likely to be hijacked than narrow-bodied, single-aisle aircraft. As of this writing, no multi-aisle plane has ever been hijacked, perhaps because hijackers would have difficulty maintaining control of the passengers on such planes.

Passengers in first-class sections are generally treated more harshly in a hijacking situation than those farther back. Passengers in aisle seats are more likely to be singled out by hijackers than those in other seats.

Some airlines have never been targeted by hijackers, perhaps because their home countries maintain neutral postures in world politics.

8

GOING BY SHIP

Traveling by water is a marvelous alternative, whether you seek adventure or luxurious relaxation, or if you fear flying or suffer unduly from jet lag. Today we have ocean liners that resemble small cities, enormous ships that steam past the once-fearsome Straits of Magellan or up the glacier-bordered Inland Passage without a break in the luxury service or lavish entertainment. Visions of acres of deck chairs, top-quality performers, fresh sea air, and the chance to view porpoises or flying fish combine to draw the traveler who can afford it to an ocean voyage purely for fun. Yet you can also book passage on a rugged freighter or a chartered sailboat. Most of this chapter is about travel on an oceangoing passenger vessel, with an introductory emphasis on the cruise as a vacation option, and a short concluding section on freighter travel.

THREE WAYS TO TRAVEL BY SHIP

Of the three most common ways to travel by ship, each offers a different type of atmosphere and level of activity, not to mention different types of fellow passengers.

Transoceanic Voyage. This generally attracts an older, more moneyed, sophisticated, worldly clientele, and the shipboard activities will reflect the intellectual, cultural, and social demands of these customers.

Cruise. These passengers aren't necessarily less affluent or sophisticated, but they seek a more casual, totally relaxing experience (fun, entertainment, and a variety of people and activities).

Freighter. Usually your fellow passengers aren't looking to catch some rays or learn volleyball; they pay by the day to accompany a cargo vessel and her crew on a voyage that could begin in Chicago and end in Amsterdam, or start in New York and wind up in Hong Kong. A freighter doesn't offer the amenities and amusements of a passenger vessel.

CRUISES

Long considered the bastion of the rich and famous, cruise vacations are now more popular than ever because of attractive pricing, special deals, and a myriad of possible destination and shipboard activities. Where else can a smart vacation shopper get transportation, accommodations, all meals, and every conceivable kind of entertainment, all for one prepaid price? Your choices and the cost can vary from an around-the-world-in-ninety-days junket to an eight-hour excursion up the Mississippi River.

Every ship offers its passengers many choices in activities, meals and entertainment, sports and recreational facilities, and social gatherings. There's something for everyone: the young married couple, singles, children, and the retired. No matter how much you pay for your cabin, you're entitled to the same amenities as every other passenger. And because you pay in advance, there are very few surprises or hidden expenses.

Check with your travel agent if you think a cruise vacation might suit you. Before you go, look over the travel section of your Sunday paper and various travel magazines to familiarize yourself with special promotions, cruise themes, and ports of call. And don't forget your alma mater: your university or college may offer cruises that explore a certain part of the world and feature explanatory lectures by college professors on the art, archaeology, and history of the area. Solicit your travel agent's opinion on various ships and cruise lines; if your agent can't answer your specific questions, then you should be directed to someone who can. You need to know all the latest deals, price breaks, special excursions, renovation plans, and which ship or ships will be best for you and your situation.

Things to keep in mind as you plan a cruise vacation include how long you want to cruise, how much you can reasonably afford to spend per person, what specific ports you do (or don't) want to see, and how flexible you can be about where you go and what ship you go on. There are as many choices as there are destinations and ships taking passengers, but if you consider the following points, it may be easier to narrow them down.

✓ Longer cruises (more than seven to ten days) are generally more formal in style and atmosphere. Shorter trips (overnight to a week or ten days) are generally more casual, and are often known as "fun ship" cruises. Accordingly, longer cruises tend to attract an older, more mature, more distinguished clientele, while shorter cruises are a haven for younger people and families.

✓ When you first see the cost for a cruise vacation, it may seem like a staggering amount of money. But remember that the price represents your total vacation expense, including transportation, accommodations, activities, and entertainment. Your out-of-pocket expenses will include tips to ship personnel at the end of the voyage (more on that later), any items you buy on board or ashore, and any shore excursions you take. If you do some quick calculations, you'll find that a cruise vacation is comparable in price to most pay-as-you-go land vacations.

✓ You make your own decisions on a cruise vacation. You can take advantage of the many activities or sit in a lounge chair for a week and soak up the sun. You're free to explore any ports your ship calls at, but it's up to you. Some cruise vacations don't make any port stops at all; some may stop at a number of ports, just long enough for you to go sightseeing; and some may spend equal amounts of time on the ocean and in port. Check the cruise itinerary to get the specifics about length and kind of port stops and whether they cost extra.

✓ Advance planning is as important to a successful cruise as to any other vacation. If you select and book a cruise early enough, and if you don't mind where your cabin is, you can save a lot. The first cabins to be booked on many cruises are either the most expensive or the least expensive. Since every passenger is entitled to the same service and offerings, you could realize significant savings by choosing a less-expensive cabin.

✓ Some cruise lines offer discounts to passengers who book "early." Your travel agent will know of any such deals, which may even be advertised in newspapers and magazines.

✓ A travel agent may try to sell you a package for more than your budget. Listen to the pitch, but be firm about your requirements. Make it clear that you want the most vacation for the least expense.

Be Flexible and Save

If you can be flexible as to where you go and what ship you go on, you can save money. Some cruise lines offer great deals to people who will fill the empty cabins on various ships and cruises. It works something like this: You decide the price range and the ship, and the cruise line decides which cruise to put you on; or you decide the price range and the cruise, and the cruise line assigns you to a ship. The savings can be considerable because cruise lines want their ships to be as full as possible before they set sail.

✓ Ask about any "fly free" (or practically free) deals that the cruise lines offer to make it easy for you to reach the port of departure. It's common practice now for cruise lines to offer round-trip airfare to passengers for free or at a greatly reduced rate.

✓ Ask what the fare would be for children who accompany adults or for a large cabin accommodating, for example, four people.

✓ Ask about any special promotions for the area or type of cruise that interests you.

CROSSING THE OCEAN BY SHIP

Whether you're afraid of flying or you just want to experience the old-fashioned style and luxury of a transatlantic crossing, you'll be glad to know that the *Queen Elizabeth 2* is still sailing, taking five days to travel between New York and Southampton, England. The *QE2* offers special deals, such as its Matched Crossings program, which gives you round-trip passage at a one-way price. Even with such a deal, however, the fare ranges between five and ten times that of flying.

After you've chosen your cruise or crossing date, you'll choose a cabin or cabins (see below) and be asked to leave a deposit that represents a percentage of the total fare. This confirms your spot and reserves your cabin (or at least a cabin in the price range you've chosen). You'll have to pay the remainder of the ticket price at some point before departure, and some lines ask you to pay in full when you book your ticket. If you haven't yet been assigned a cabin, you'll be given a cabin number when your entire fare has been paid.

Examine your ticket when you receive it: confirm the ship, the cabin assignment, the date of departure, and the point of departure. The ticket will state the cruise line's policy on everything from luggage restrictions to what will happen if the cruise is unexpectedly cut short. The ticket is really a contract — read all the fine print so that you understand what to expect from the cruise lines and what they expect from you as a passenger.

Red Tape
No passport is necessary for cruises to the Bahamas, the Caribbean, Mexico, and Canada. If you'll be sailing to Mexico, you may need a Mexican Tourist Card. You should obtain one, if necessary, from your travel agent or the nearest Mexican consulate before you leave. If you'll be visiting any countries other than these, then you must have a passport and any necessary visas, just like a land traveler.

The ticket outlines the policy on passenger cancellations. If you have to cancel and you can let the cruise line know well enough in advance, you probably won't be penalized with cancellation charges, and you should receive back the entire price of your ticket. But the closer you get to the departure date, the greater the chance that the cruise line will keep a portion of your fare, as a deterrent against capricious reservations. Unlike airlines, cruise companies cannot overbook because passengers can't wait for the next available berth, and they ask for payment to reserve a place for every passenger.

Certainly emergencies arise, and you might have to change your plans. If illness intervenes and your doctor will verify that, the cruise line may give you a full refund. But when you book a cruise or crossing it's assumed that you understand the provisions under which the ticket was sold.

Many travel agents sell trip cancellation insurance for a small fee, which will protect you if you can't make the trip. Trip insurance is an especially good idea if you're traveling by ship, not only because you generally pay your fare in advance, but because cancellation penalties can be severe. The ticket, and your travel agent, will give you all the specifics, but the burden is on you to know the cancellation policy for the trip you book.

YOUR CABIN

Choosing a cabin can be less mysterious with the help of a travel agent. Realize ahead of time that your accommodations will be small — a lot smaller than they appear in the brochure, and less than half the size of a conventional hotel room. If the cruise line is true to its advertising, you won't be spending much time there anyway, except to sleep and change clothes, but be prepared for cabin intimacy.

The cabins on most older ships are slightly larger than those on most new ships, and a bit more gracious and elegant. Newer ships offer cabins that are practically identical in size and shape, unless you book a suite or a deluxe accommodation.

You pay more for a cabin that is closer to the public rooms and main decks. If you don't mind walking up a flight or two of stairs or taking an elevator, you can get the same cabin for less.

It's now standard for each cabin to have bathroom facilities, but the bathroom will be even smaller, proportionally, than your cabin.

Realistically, only one person can use it at a time. There probably won't be a bathtub, just a shower stall.

You will also have some drawer space, a dressing table, a closet, and beds. The beds, as you'll see in the ship's brochure, are most likely twin beds. The floor plans on some ships will allow you to push the two beds together, but that may drastically reduce your maneuverability. Also offered, in tourist class or in cabins for four passengers, are bunk beds and Pullman beds that flip up during the day to give you more room. If you want a double or queen-sized bed, you'll need a larger room, which will cost more money.

Find out how close your cabin is to the public rooms. If you like to get to bed early, you won't want to be near the disco or bar, and if you like to sleep late, you shouldn't be near the dining room or uppermost decks. Rooms near stairs or the elevators may be noisy when people go to and from their cabins, as are rooms near the ship's engines and the kitchen.

If you think you may get seasick, book a cabin away from the bow, on the lower decks, and toward the center of the ship (not looking out at the sea). A good analogy is a tall tree swaying in the wind: the tree sways less lower down on the trunk and in the middle. Of course, all modern cruise ships have stabilizers to lessen the effects of rough waters.

Inside rooms may be a bit darker and perhaps a little smaller than outside rooms, but they're generally less expensive.

Outside rooms have a window or porthole (sealed shut because of the air conditioning) and will cost more. Some outside rooms have portholes that face a deck or promenade, and passengers will be walking and talking past your window for the entire trip. There are of course curtains, but if you appreciate both privacy and outside rooms, you should make sure that your window offers a view only of the ocean, and not of other passengers.

ⅢⅡ WHAT TO TAKE ⅢⅡ

You pack for a cruise or crossing in much the same way as you would for any other vacation. First of all, do a little research about where you're going and what kind of climate to expect, both in port and on the water.

A good, comfortable pair of shoes is as important on a cruise vacation as on a land vacation — you'll do more than your share of walking even if you never leave the ship.

The night air on the water can be cool, and so can the interior of the ship, so be sure to bring at least one jacket or sweater to fight off the chills.

Try to coordinate your wardrobe to minimize the need for cleaning and laundry services. If your trip is a short one, your clothes may not need cleaning. If you're thinking of laundering items yourself, remember that you won't have much space in your cabin for a travel clothesline.

Certainly you'll want to bring sportswear and one or more dressy outfits: for women this could mean a formal dress or gown, and for men it usually means just a dark business suit. Very few cruises are so formal that men should pack a tuxedo and women their ball gowns, but your travel agent will know the level of formality on your particular cruise.

Check the ship's brochure to learn the electrical compatibility with your various traveling appliances (hair dryers, razors, curling irons). Travel irons are prohibited on many ships not only because they require more electricity, but because they pose a tremendous fire risk. Depending on where your ship was built and the countries it primarily services, you may or may not need a voltage converter. If promotional materials don't cover this, be sure to get an answer from your travel agent or someone at the cruise line.

Any luggage you take on a cruise will be subject to abuse — the same abuse it suffers on planes, in cabs, and on trains, perhaps even more so. Pack your things in durable luggage. Hard items, such as shoes, should line the outside (near the zipper) of your bag. Protect breakables in zip-closure bags.

ⅠⅡⅢ MEALS AND ACTIVITIES ⅠⅡⅢ

On a cruise or crossing you'll be offered more in the way of food and activity than any mortal being could eat or absorb. You'll surely be astounded by the number and variety of each.

The larger ships offer two sittings for every meal, with approximately two hours separating each sitting. The second sitting usually attracts a more gregarious, fun-loving group. You can often request a sitting when you book or pay for your tickets, and you may even be able to get your table assignment.

Approach the dining room steward as soon as you get a chance, if you haven't been assigned to a table by the time you arrive on ship. You can choose a table for two, four, eight, or, in some cases, ten or twelve. You can ask to be seated with traveling companions, you can ask to sit at a large table, or you can ask for a table for two. One frequent cruiser we know recommends choosing a table for eight — there's sure to be someone you hit it off with. Whatever size table you choose, arrive promptly for each meal. No one at your table will be served until everyone has arrived.

If you feel dissatisfied with your table, ask the maitre d'hotel for a change. Such a request will usually be honored when it's made persuasively and graciously.

You must pay for any wine or drinks with your meal, but that's all the cash you'll need in the dining room.

No tips are necessary until the end of the trip, when you may see fit to tip the dining room steward and the sommelier for their care and attention.

The menu for each meal will keep every palate satisfied and intrigued, and there may be open buffets at other times of the day — midafternoon for those who missed lunch, and very late at night for those who have been socializing until the wee hours of the morning.

If you have special dietary needs (kosher, low-salt, low-sugar, allergies), let the dining room steward know as soon as you arrive.

Shipboard Activities

Activities may range from the Captain's Dinner or evening gala to lectures, aerobics classes, and game competitions. The ship will publish a daily calendar of events so that you know when every meal is offered and what social, recreational, and entertainment activities are taking place that day. Cruise ship fitness facilities, in particular, grow more elaborate every year.

HEALTH

Every floating passenger vessel is required to have a doctor on board. Some will also have a number of nurses, and the largest ships have medical facilities more like a small hospital than an infirmary. There might be a small fee for a visit to the doctor's office, or you may be asked to pay only for any medicines that are dispensed. Bring along some money, just in case.

The ship's doctor will be available to treat most minor ailments, and in the event of a medical emergency will refer you to a specialist at the nearest port. Remember, though, that medical services and resources aboard a cruise ship are necessarily limited. The American Medical Association is working to establish international standards for medical care on cruises.

Seasickness can afflict even the experienced oceangoer. There's no need to suffer long: the ship's physician can give you a prescription to provide some relief. Whatever else you may do when, or if, you get seasick, don't drink alcohol in an attempt to forget how rotten you feel. Alcohol will only add to your instability, disorientation, and nausea. Try a good old-fashioned cure: Go out on deck for a few hours, breathe some fresh air, and gaze at the reason for your malaise until you get your sea legs and your stomach calms down.

Pack plenty of sun lotion and sunscreen. Those who cruise in the winter months often get badly sunburned.

ᴵᴵᴵ ᴀT THᴇ ᴇNᴅ Oᖴ THᴇ VOᵾᴀGᴇ ᴵᴵᴵ

You are encouraged to tip those members of the ship's staff who have offered you help, advice, and cheerful, professional service. The cruise information brochure should mention a recommended tip for your cabin steward, dining room waiter, and busboy. Typically, the minimum tip for a cabin steward is three dollars per person per day; for a dining room waiter or steward, three dollars per day for each person served; and for the busboy, one dollar a day. Wine stewards or sommeliers and bartenders are tipped fifteen percent of the cost of the wine or drinks you consumed.

Any person who gives you extra-ordinary service deserves a more generous tip, and perhaps a letter of thanks.

As the end of the voyage nears, the cruise director will offer a session to the passengers on debarkation procedures and will provide luggage tags and customs forms. Attach these luggage tags to your bags and leave all but your carry-on luggage outside your door on the night before you arrive at the final port. Your steward will see that your baggage gets safely to the deck.

Getting Through Customs

Customs should be little more than a formality. Keep all your receipts and pack your purchases near the top of your bags in case they must be inspected. Fill in your customs declaration forms as instructed by the cruise director and hand them to the customs official as your turn arrives. See Chapter 16 for information on customs duties. If you have any questions or fears, ask the cruise director or your cabin steward before you get to customs.

ⅢⅢ SPECIAL CRUISES ⅢⅢ

Cruise vacations or crossings are not limited to the young-adult, able-bodied, married crowd. Cruising is open to practically anyone who has the desire and money to go, regardless of marital status or age.

Many cruise lines encourage you to bring along the kids by offering greatly discounted fares for children who accompany a full-paying adult. Get a recommendation from a friend or travel agent about cruises suitable for children and families. But be aware that, in the vernacular of the passenger ship industry, "children" can be defined as any young person under the age of twelve or fourteen or seventeen — quite a range. Ask specifically if the cruise you have in mind is going to be right for *your* children — whether they are four and six or fifteen and seventeen. Keep in mind that the cruise industry will probably carry a full children's staff only during the summer and school vacation periods.

Some cruises are better suited to families and children than others — shorter cruises will be more attractive to children and are more likely to have a children's cruise director. Before you commit yourself to bringing the kids, check to be sure that the trip you have in mind offers a full calendar of children's events and will meet your children's needs and schedule.

The singles crowd is flocking to the "fun ships" not only because a cruise is a popular vacation, but also because it offers opportunities to meet all kinds of other interesting people — single and not. Cruise lines that are known for their "fun ships" will cater to the singles crowd, with good deals and imaginative bookings. Sadly, however, a single passenger often must pay as much as double the fare for a cabin. Many lines will assign you another single roommate if you want to avoid this surcharge. If you're lucky, they won't be able to fill the space — at no extra cost to you.

The second sitting may be more enjoyable for a single person, as those at the second sitting are more likely to be adventurous and outgoing. A table of eight or more will give you a chance to meet a number of different people right from the start.

A cruise vacation can also be ideal for the older or disabled traveler. If you tell your travel agent of your needs, together you'll be able to come up with a ship and cruise that will be right for you. Newer ships have wider passageways, halls, and doorways, and are more accessible to wheelchairs. Wheelchair passengers are asked to have an able-bodied person accompany them. Book a cabin on an upper deck near the elevators.

ⅼⅼⅼⅼ **FREIGHTERS** ⅼⅼⅼⅼ

Freighter travel is for the unhurried and the unimpatient. Some travel agents will be able to help you book a trip as a passenger on a cargo vessel, but you'll be better off contacting the shipping lines directly (see Useful Addresses, page 217).

Freighter World Cruises, for one, offers crossings on its cargo vessels at a low price. They take eleven to nineteen days, each way. The ships leave New York and head south to Norfolk, Virginia, and Savannah, Georgia, before heading across the Pond to Italian, French, and Spanish ports.

The itinerary for a freighter is usually quite tentative in the early stages of the trip. All you may know for sure is where you're departing from and where you hope to end up. The trip could be two weeks longer or shorter than anticipated, and you may stop at a dozen different ports along the way. Before you buy a ticket, try as best you can to get a complete itinerary. It's assumed that a passenger on a cargo ship isn't in a great hurry to get somewhere, and that if the plans of the captain change along the way, it won't make too much difference to you.

Most cargo ships don't carry any more than twelve passengers in addition to the officers and crew. You'll get to know the officers and crew well because you eat every meal together, and they may join you in cards, chess, backgammon, or other recreation. You'll have to entertain yourself during the working day. Be sure you know how much time you have to explore while the ship is in port.

The passenger quarters on most freighters can be surprisingly spacious and comfortable. Be sure to pack a casual wardrobe that can be washed in the sink (there may be washing machines, but don't count on it) and hung to dry. Although you probably won't use a travel clothesline on a cruise or crossing, you'll be glad to have one on a freighter voyage.

Passengers on a freighter pay by the day rather than in advance — probably because some passengers have been known to disembark at the strangest places. When you make your reservations, ask about the deposit and about how you should pay your fare if your destination isn't definite. You can pay anywhere from $40 to more than $100 per day — considerably less than you would pay a cruise line. At those prices, and with all the incredible ports there are to visit, there's a freighter voyage for every budget and imagination.

You won't have much in the way of shipboard entertainment, because the freighter's main function is to transport cargo. Life at sea can become tedious — be sure to pack reading and writing materials and portable games.

Tips are smaller, because passenger services on a freighter don't compare to those on a cruise ship. On the last day of your trip, you should tip 5 percent of your total fare, divided equally between your stateroom and dining room stewards. If you're on a longer voyage, tip weekly.

For the More Adventuresome

You can go down to the harbor and ask around for a ship that's going where you want to go, in some parts of the world. This method of freighter travel is much less reliable than arranging your trip in advance, and you travel at your own risk. A friend and I once took a cargo ship from Barbados to Trinidad. After a raucous going-away party, the captain and the entire crew went to bed, and the huge ship was steered through the night by the deaf second mate, without benefit of radio or radar. Miraculously, the ship arrived safely in Port of Spain at dawn — but if it hadn't, the two passengers would have had no recourse.

‖‖‖ 9 ‖‖‖

GETTING AROUND

Most important, in navigating in an unfamiliar place, is to orient yourself quickly. Purchase a map of the city or country ahead of time and become familiar with it. Circle the places you plan to visit.

Whether you'll be driving or taking public transportation, try to get into the habit of thinking in kilometers, if that's the standard measure in the country you're visiting. It's much more efficient than constantly converting. (In case you've forgotten, however, a kilometer is 0.62 miles.)

‖‖ DRIVING ‖‖

The United States is ideal for car travel, the way Europe is ideal for trains. In this country, take the back roads, away from the Interstate Highway System. Try following one highway across broad stretches of the country — what remains of old U.S. Route 66, or U.S. 1 up the Atlantic Coast, or U.S. 2, which travels east-west just south of and parallel to the Canadian border. (See also Chapter 18, "Traveling with Children.")

Before deciding to drive abroad, remember that in a foreign country a private car can be very isolating. Your reality is the interior of the car and the dynamics of your group, more than the culture of the country. Gasoline costs much more in most other countries. You have to find parking. And you have to cope with unfamiliar driving customs and traffic laws.

But a car does have the advantage of being your home-away-from-home. A group can travel more cheaply in a car. You can bring more gear, such as a portable crib and stroller for a baby. If you're on a tight budget, you can combine transportation and lodging costs by sleeping in your car at campgrounds. And you can go where you want, when you want.

In all of Western Europe except Spain, Americans can legally drive with just their own state driver's license. Spain and many countries outside Western Europe require that visitors carry an International Driver's Permit. This can be obtained inexpensively from any affiliate of the American Automobile Association (you need not be a member).

I don't recommend driving a car in Asia, unless it's a Jeep in which you expect to tackle the Himalayas or other rugged areas. (Motorcycles make more sense but are also more dangerous.) Few traffic jams can compare with the conglomeration of vehicles at a Calcutta crossroad — wagons drawn by water buffalo and horses, honking trucks, taxis, rickshaws, aggressive private cars, motorcycles, and bicycles — not to mention pedestrians and, always, the wild card: a holy cow wandering through. To make things more confusing, you must drive on the left.

Picnics are one of the pleasures of car travel. Get yourself some picnic equipment (see Chapter 11, "Dining"), and when you pass through a small town in late morning, purchase fresh bread, local cheese, milk, cereal, tea or instant coffee, fruit, vegetables, cold cuts, nuts, yogurt, and dish soap. Or you can keep it simpler. My husband and I once hitchhiked through England and Wales, every day buying a loaf of local bread, some local cheese, and a little jar of mustard for a picnic. Every village offered its own unique product, and all were delicious.

If you have a cooler you'll be able to eat marvelously; if you have a stove you'll even be able to make a pot of tea in that nice spot you found off the side of the road with a view of Loch Lomond.

Make sure you place within easy reach the things you may need quickly. I keep easily accessible a first-aid kit (see Chapter 4, "Health"), swimsuits, cameras, binoculars, sturdy walking shoes, and sweaters. All of these could be packed together in one duffel bag.

When spending only one or two nights on the road, pack a small bag with your overnight needs so that you won't have to bring all of your luggage into your hotel or motel.

Your vehicle will be more stable if you carry less on top of your car, and more inside it. Keep the center of gravity low by packing heavy items inside the car and light things on top.

ⅲ RENTING CARS AND OTHER OPTIONS ⅲ

It's generally cheaper to arrange for a car rental from the United States. The best deal is to rent a car by the week with unlimited mileage. Remember that in addition to the rental cost you'll have to pay the collision damage waiver (CDW) supplement of about $90 per week (as of this printing). You can lease, rent, or buy a car in Europe through Europe by Car (see Useful Addresses, page 217).

You need to know insurance requirements in order to drive a new car around Europe (the cost varies according to the make of car), and your car must carry a first-aid kit and have a "Danger" triangle on the back. (Note that if you bring a new car back to the United States, you'll have to prove that its emissions level meets American standards.)

Leasing can be cheaper than renting. A minimum period (two weeks or seventeen days) usually applies. If you lease a new car, you pay no mileage charge, and taxes and insurance are included in the cost. After driving a thousand kilometers, however, you must take the car in for service, which means you could be without it for a day.

Rental agencies can have very different prices, even in the same location.

In the United States, small local rental agencies are cheaper than the big-name places.

Pick up your car somewhere other than the airport and you'll probably save money. Some agencies provide shuttle service to and from the airport.

Further Information

See also Questions to Ask Before Renting a Car, page 205.

Some rental agencies in Europe will not rent cars to people over seventy or under twenty-five.

Gasoline ("petrol") costs at least twice as much in Europe as in the United States, although the small European cars get excellent mileage. Inquire whether you can rent a car that runs on diesel, which is much cheaper than gasoline — at this writing, two-thirds the cost.

It's expensive, and sometimes prohibited, to take a rental car on a ferry between England and Ireland or the Continent. I recommend renting a separate car on the other side.

▓ FEELING SAFE AND SECURE ▓ ON THE ROAD

When driving in another country, you must keep your wits about you — car accidents are the leading cause of death for travelers.

The biggest challenge is driving on the left, as is the custom in a good part of the world (especially in countries that are or were part of the British Commonwealth). Many travelers find shifting with the left hand most difficult. (The clutch and the brake are in the same location as in American cars.)

Driving on the Left

Allow at least a week to get accustomed to driving on the left. Be prepared, however, for lapses anytime in the first six months. Two tips:

- Consciously focus whenever you make a left or right turn.

- Traffic circles (called roundabouts in Great Britain and Ireland) are especially nerve-wracking. If you feel panicky, stay in the inner lane of the circle, going around as many times as it takes until you're calm and ready to exit the circle. Most other cars remain in the outer lane.

Beware: drivers in many other countries tend to drive more aggressively than Americans do, whether on city streets or on the famous German Autobahn. You'll witness other drivers continually taking risks: passing on narrow, winding roads, charging through red lights, driving at 90 miles (145 kilometers) an hour on freeways. The Autobahn is one of the world's most superb highways, well engineered and direct, but it has no speed limit. Many tragic accidents occur on this highway.

Be sure to wear your seat belt and try to drive slowly enough to stay calm and collected.

Be aware of crosswalks. In many cities, both in this country and elsewhere, you must stop the moment someone steps onto a crosswalk (called a "zebra crossing" in England). If in doubt about local regulations, stop anyway. It's a much-appreciated courtesy.

You must prepay at the entrance to the motorway (superhighway) in some European countries. Make sure you know your exit point before you arrive at the entrance toll booth. (If necessary, you can point out your route on your map to the toll booth attendant.)

International Highway Signs

No entry   *No waiting*   *No U turns*   *Speed limit*

(Right) curve   *Intersection*   *Dangerous curves*   *Railroad crossing*

All vehicles prohibited   *Danger*

Be sure to leave enough time at the end of the day to find lodging and a restaurant, if you haven't booked your hotel ahead of time. Booking ahead is wise, especially if you're traveling in high season or expecting to arrive very late. (See Chapter 10, "Lodging.")

TRAINS

I once had the travel experience of my life when I rode with a friend fourth class on a train across Brazil and Bolivia for a week. Instead of riding in a swanky passenger car with seats and air conditioning, we sat with dozens of local passengers on the floor in boxcars, with the doors wide open to the rolling countryside, sleeping in sleeping bags at night and eating at the little stations. If you're young and hardy, you'll never forget the experience of how local people travel long distances in Third World countries.

You must stay alert, because certain amenities you might expect may be missing. When my friend and I got off at one station, the train started to leave without any whistle or announcement. We had to run and actually hop the train, assisted by many helping hands; otherwise, we would have been left behind without our belongings.

Amtrak offers very attractive family packages, comfortable trains, and scenic routes in the United States. For current prices, call the toll-free number (see Useful Addresses, page 217). You can book eleven months ahead or up to the date of departure, if there's room.

Budget travel through Europe is available with a dizzying variety of train passes, ranging from Ireland's Emerald Isle Card to the Greek Flexipass. For an excellent, detailed comparison of costs and routes, see *Rick Steves' Europe through the Back Door* (Santa Fe: John Muir Publications, 1996). Many rail passes must be purchased in the United States.

The Eurailpass is still an excellent deal, if you wish to visit a lot of countries in Europe. You don't need a reservation; you simply board the train, sit in an unreserved seat, and show the conductor your pass. Note, however, that you should buy the Eurailpass before you leave the United States — it's expensive and not widely available abroad. Here are some tips regarding its use:

✓ The Eurailpass is valid for Austria, Belgium, Denmark, Finland, France, Germany, Greece, Hungary, Ireland, Italy, Luxembourg, the Netherlands, Norway, Portugal, Spain, Sweden, and Switzerland. Note that although you can use the pass in Ireland, it isn't valid in England, Scotland, or Wales, where you need a BritRail Pass. Obtain information on both passes from your travel agent, Eurailpass, or the Forsyth Travel Library (see Useful Addresses).

✓ A single Eurailpass gives you unlimited first-class rail travel. It's also good for many scheduled boat trips on the Danube and the Rhine, steamers on Swiss lakes, and ferries between France and Ireland, Sweden and Denmark, and Greece and Italy. It's issued for fifteen days, twenty-one days, or one, two, or three months. Children under twelve can obtain a Eurailpass for half the adult fare; children under four travel free on European trains.

✓ The Eurailpass becomes valid on the first day you use it. You can get it stamped beforehand for the correct starting date, if you expect you'll be in a hurry when you get to the station. Be sure to get the stamp before you board the train; otherwise, you may pay a penalty. Once your pass is stamped, you can simply board the train and flash the pass.

✓ Do not purchase a Eurailpass if you plan to take a train to one place and stay there. The pass is for travelers who want to cover a lot of territory in a limited time.

✓ The Eurailpass also entitles the holder to reduced rates for car rentals in France; reduced fares on some Europabus lines in Belgium, France, Italy, and Switzerland; and free passage on trains between certain airports and cities (Amsterdam, Barcelona, Brussels, Düsseldorf, Frankfurt, Paris, and Zurich).

✔ Even with a Eurailpass, you must secure a reservation in advance if you want to be sure of getting a seat. A reservation is compulsory for travel in sleepers. In Spain, you must have a reservation or you won't be allowed to board an express train. You may also reserve a seat in the dining car.

The Eurail Youthpass, for people under twenty-six, provides one to two months of unlimited second-class rail travel. At this writing, however, children under twelve travel cheaper on a half-fare Eurailpass.

The Europass covers travel between three to five adjacent countries: France, Germany, Italy, Spain, and Switzerland. Other countries may be added at additional cost.

Special Train Pass Discounts

If you are a student or a senior, you can make arrangements for special discounts through a recognized organization, such as the Council on International Educational Exchange, the International Youth Hostel Organization, or the American Association of Retired Persons. (Refer to Useful Addresses.) Have your membership card with you.

The Eurail Saverpass is for a group of three or more companions (or a group of two or more from October through March). Valid for fifteen days of unlimited first-class rail travel, it's an excellent deal for adults traveling together, but for families it still can't match the value of the original Eurailpass.

If all of your train travel will be done in one country, purchase a cheaper pass just for that country. A Swiss Holiday Card, for example, is at this writing a little more than half the cost of a Eurailpass for fifteen days. Contact the Forsyth Travel Library (see Useful Addresses).

If you'll be taking trains in Europe, study or purchase a Thomas Cook Continental Timetable to help you plan your itinerary. Order an up-to-date copy from the Forsyth Travel Library.

In Europe, a sleeper is a bedroom, and a couchette is an open bunk (with pillow and blanket but no privacy). You can request a smoking or a nonsmoking compartment. The price of the sleeper varies according to type of accommodation and distance traveled; for the couchette you pay a flat charge per night. You'll probably have to reserve either of these at least a day in advance, but if you haven't, ask the conductor. There may be one available.

Take a blanket or extra sweaters for night train travel, especially in the spring or fall. In winter, in contrast, train cars can be stiflingly hot.

Take a picnic basket or lunchbox for the kids. In many countries, vendors appear at the windows during station stops and offer snacks for sale. In Third World countries this can be a thriving business. You'll be offered local delicacies and a cup of sweet tea or coffee through the train window.

Save Money by Traveling at Night

Reserve a berth and you'll get both your transportation and your bed for one price. Inquire when you make your reservation whether you must also reserve a meal.

Have extra soap, a towel, and toilet paper with you and accessible if you're traveling for a few days on a train.

Be sure to remain in the correct seat in the correct car, if you've reserved a seat. Otherwise, your car may be shunted off to a different city — or country.

Examine your ticket to make sure the correct portion has been taken when the conductor stamps your ticket. Keep your ticket; in some cities and countries you need it when you get off.

When you arrive at the station, always look immediately for the poster or computerized timetable showing you which track your train is on. Most European train stations have a diagram of each train showing the location of each car, so that you'll know exactly where on the platform to stand. Look also for "pictograms" showing where to find restaurants, rest rooms, baggage areas, and so forth.

Many terminals throughout the world have a "Left Luggage" storage facility. If you can find such a service, you'll be free of your luggage for some sightseeing. Make sure you retrieve the luggage in plenty of time for your departure. These are popular services, and if you're late you can face a long line of anxious travelers and cross clerks.

Some European stations will forward your luggage to meet you at the train station in another city, thus freeing you to travel unencumbered. This usually takes a few days. Some stations can send your bags from the station to the airport, and, in Switzerland, even onto your plane.

⑾ BUSES ⑾

Buses can be exhausting, but they're the cheapest form of motorized transportation and one of the very best ways to penetrate a country and meet people. In some parts of the world buses are packed to the gills with people and then career up mountain passes and over suspension bridges with the radio blasting and the horn honking. In other countries they're comfortable, air-conditioned, serene.

In the United States ask about bargains. Various bus lines, including Greyhound (see Useful Addresses), offer reduced fares, sightseeing packages, and special passes.

On domestic buses children under two travel free; from two to twelve years old, they ride for half fare. There are special rates available for disabled travelers, clergy, members of the armed forces, and groups.

In London and Paris you can prebook unlimited subway and city bus travel vouchers along with rail travel bargains.

⑾ BOATS ⑾

Take a boat wherever possible — through the canals of Bangkok or Venice or Southern France, up the west coast of Canada to Alaska, across the English Channel, around Boston Harbor. Cities seem to look their best and make most sense when seen from the water.

The Eurailpass and its offshoots will cover many types of boat trips in Europe, including steamers and ferries.

If you're interested in chartering a sailboat in the Caribbean, contact the Caribbean Yacht Company, located in St. Thomas; Nautor's Swan, in St. Martin; or Moorings, with six bases in the Caribbean. Refer to Useful Addresses for their toll-free phone numbers.

⑾ GETTING AROUND IN A CITY ⑾

Use your city map to plan your route to places you want to see. A tourist office will usually have a map of the city bus or subway system.

If the language is unfamiliar, have the hotel desk clerk write down the name of your hotel. If you get lost, you can simply show the slip of paper to a cab driver and be taken back to your hotel without too much trouble.

Consider taking an orientation tour your first day in an unfamiliar city, even if you plan just to stroll around. It will point out places of interest, give you an idea of layout and neighborhoods, and provide some interesting background and history. Then when you're ready to negotiate the city by yourself, you'll have some sense of distances and routes.

City buses and subways in some European cities run on an honor system. You buy a ticket, board the bus, and punch your own ticket. No one routinely checks, but there are serious penalties for people found with unpunched tickets. In the Lyons, France, métro, for example, random checks are made, and those without punched tickets are punished.

Certain seats on public transport are reserved for pregnant women, war veterans, and disabled people. If people are standing and there's an empty seat, check for a sign indicating restricted use.

ⅢⅠ W A L K I N G ⅢⅠ

Trek in India or Nepal, hill-walk in Scotland, amble through the Alps, walk from village to village in South America, prowl Paris or London. . . . If you're strong and have time, walking is without doubt the finest way to travel, especially in the Third World, where you'll have a lot of interesting company. In India, my husband and I walked for a week through the Himalayas with a *sadhu* (holy man), and my images of those dramatic mountains are forever brightened by the memory of our companion's warm humor and resourcefulness.

Wear a pair of sturdy, well-broken-in walking shoes, and take along a good map, extra pairs of cotton socks, and as light a pack as possible. Dress in layers, so that you can strip down as the day warms up. It's very soothing to bathe your feet and change into a fresh pair of socks if you should come upon a stream or well at midday.

Don't Overestimate

Although humans are technically capable of walking three miles an hour, walking twenty miles in one day with a pack can be quite arduous, especially over hills. Be conservative in your estimates about how far you can go, and you'll have time to relax.

Take a poncho that covers you and your knapsack, and if you choose to wear sneakers, have with you some rubber galoshes in case you end up walking in the rain. There's nothing so uncomfortable as sloshing along in wet sneakers — unless it's putting them on again the next morning.

Have a good breakfast before you set out, and bring with you some trail food ("gorp") for a midmorning break. Stop at a grocery to buy a picnic lunch, and then walk on to another village for supper and sleep.

ⅢⅠ G O I N G B Y B I K E ⅢⅠ

Americans don't often consider the bicycle as a serious mode of transportation. Yes, you need to be in good shape, and you can pack only as much as you can carry, but if you really want to see the countryside and meet the locals, going by bike will provide the greatest opportunities. And, of course, it's the most inexpensive way to go, next to walking.

Bike Bag

Make a "bike bag," if you can't find a box. It looks like a big fabric envelope and should accommodate the bike with its front wheel removed, have a big flap on the outside, and have either an inside pocket for the front wheel or a length of fabric in which to wrap it. Insert a plastic spacer (available from a bike shop) between the front forks to prevent crushing. Sew on a handle or shoulder strap, and you're done. Use fabric such as parachute cloth, which will fold easily and not take much space. Bring some rope or packing tape to secure the bike.

Purchase or rent a bike that's in good working condition. If you rent, be sure to select one that's right for your height and weight: you should just be able to touch the ground with the tip of your toe when you sit on the seat. The tires should have enough air to withstand your full weight, including your fully packed bags.

Prepare yourself physically by taking a good ride (of about ten miles) five days a week for at least three weeks prior to your departure.

Pack rain gear and sunscreen — and, of course, a good helmet.

Verify that your airline will accept your bike as an item of luggage, although most do. If you're going by air, try to obtain a shipping box from a local bike shop. (These are becoming harder to find, however, because new bikes are now being shipped wrapped in many layers of heavy plastic.)

American cyclists abroad do not feel nearly as threatened by drivers as they do at home. A common sight in almost every foreign country, bicyclists are generally treated with respect and care.

ⅲⅰ HITCHHIKING ⅲⅰ

At its best, hitchhiking is much more than just a way to get to your destination for free. It can bring great rewards, including long-lasting friendships and marvelous experiences. It lets you into people's lives and gives special insights into, and memories of, wherever you visit.

Never forget, however, that hitchhiking is extremely risky. Hitch-hikers must be very cautious and alert. They must be good at judging character, fast. They must be courteous and friendly so that the driver is glad to have picked them up, yet they must never be flirtatious. They must be able to talk their way out of difficult situations. And they must know exactly where they are going.

Certain places are considered safer for hitchhiking than others. These include Canada and Northern Europe. The United States is not a safe place to hitchhike, nor is Southern Europe.

The best combination for hitchhiking is a man and a woman. One woman alone will get a ride quickly but will continually find herself in tense or dangerous situations. Two men will find hitching together safe but very slow.

Talk to other hitchhikers about best routes, best places to stay, best "hitching posts." Some cities or routes are notoriously bad places to get a ride. The Sudbury/Sault Sainte-Marie area of Ontario is one such spot; Tok Junction, Alaska, is another. I once heard of a man and a woman, traveling separately, who got stuck in Tok Junction together for two weeks and ended up getting legally hitched — married! If you don't have that degree of flexibility, find out about such places and avoid them, either by choosing a different route or by waiting for a ride that will take you beyond them.

Think through exactly what you would do in an emergency. Women traveling together sometimes select a code word so that one can alert the other if she senses a problem.

Don't use a sign stating your destination unless you want one ride on a superhighway all the way into a big city. Not only could you wind up with a nonstop ride you don't like the looks of, but you may also miss the interesting local traffic.

119

Hitchhiking Tips

- Never hitchhike at night.
- Study a map and learn every detail of your route — towns, highway route numbers, distances, landmarks. Carry your map, folded to show the correct region, in an accessible pocket of your luggage, and keep it near you to refer to while you're riding in the car.
- Know the national and local laws regarding hitchhiking. It's nearly always forbidden (not to mention extremely dangerous) to hitchhike on limited-access, multilane highways. Stay on entrance ramps — or avoid high-speed highways entirely.
- On secondary roads, stand where you can be seen from at least two hundred feet away and where a car or truck can pull safely off the road. Intersections are ideal because the traffic slows down.
- The early hitcher gets the ride — get out there at dawn!
- Take a city bus or subway to the outskirts of town to pick up your highway.
- If there's a line of hitchhikers, go to the end of it.
- Use the proper hand signal! It varies from country to country. Notice what others do.
- Dress neatly and modestly. Wearing outlandish clothes is asking for trouble.
- Do not smoke cigarettes or sit while hitchhiking.
- Before you get into a car, ask the driver where he or she is going. Take a good look at all occupants of the car. If you don't like their looks, simply and courteously refuse the ride.
- Do not accept a ride with two or more men unless you are absolutely certain the situation is safe.
- The safest rides are with women, couples, families, and solo men. (Solo men are by far the most likely to pick you up.)
- Keep your belongings next to you, just in case you have to get out.
- Do not fall asleep in the car.
- If you begin to feel uncomfortable, ask to stop at the next service station. Say you feel carsick. Once you've stopped, take your belongings and inform the driver that you won't be going any farther.

10

LODGING

Hotels may eat up a larger piece of your budget than any other single expense (unless you're going to Asia, where the plane ticket is expensive and lodging is cheap). When traveling to foreign countries, book ahead only your first night's reservation. Once you're over there, you can find a smaller or more suitable accommodation. Small neighborhood hotels are not only inexpensive, but they also offer a truer sense of the place. In this country, it is also a good idea to reserve ahead, using a guidebook or budget motel guide.

Perhaps the most valuable service guidebooks offer is advice on lodgings. Not only do they list address, telephone, and price range, along with a brief description of facilities and ambience, but their endorsement counts as a recommendation (not a guarantee) that the place is honest and clean.

You may find, however, that you meet the same tourists over and over again — obviously they have the same criteria you do and are picking out the same hotels from the same book. To avoid feeling like part of a herd, pick up more than one guidebook. Photocopy or cut out the relevant portions and bring them along, not the entire bound books. You can toss them out as you leave the country.

Before going to less touristed areas of the world, such as South America, Africa, and the South Pacific, you may wish to avail yourself of all available guidebooks, to give yourself the maximum amount of advance information. Guidebooks are invariably excellent reading, ahead of time.

If you choose not to use a guidebook or if you find yourself way off the beaten track, here are some pointers on finding a hotel:

✓ Ask other travelers for their recommendations. They may tell you the place you're heading for that night has bedbugs, or excellent coffee, or that you'll find a better, cheaper place around the corner.

✓ When I visit a city for more than just a day or two, I may stay in one hotel the first night and then stroll around the city looking for a more appropriate place — cheaper or more luxurious, more in the center or closer to the beach.

✓ In a beach city, such as Mazatlán, Mexico, a hotel on the beach may be astoundingly expensive, but one just a block away could fall within your means.

✓ Always ask to see the room before you take it. (In many countries, this is standard.) Make sure it's clean, well equipped, and located in a satisfactory and safe part of the hotel. Check to see that the heat and/or air-conditioning actually work, that windows open and close, and, if you're in the tropics, that there are window screens. Make sure doors and windows lock. Listen to the street-noise level. If you aren't happy with the room, ask to see another one — or ask that the price be reduced.

Further Information
See also Questions to Ask When Making a Hotel Reservation, page 206.

ⅢⅡ **FIRE PRECAUTIONS** ⅢⅡ

Check to see where the fire exit is and what the fire regulations are. They should be posted on the back of the door in your room. (See also Chapter 15, "Safety and Security.")

Dear friends of mine were traveling in Scotland when they were awakened in the middle of the night by someone pounding on the door and shouting that the hotel was on fire. They left the room immediately, without shoes, glasses, money, or passports, and ran down the three flights of stairs to the ground. Within two minutes everyone had evacuated the hotel, which was totally destroyed. Miraculously, no one was caught inside.

My friends had lost everything, however, except the nightclothes they were wearing. Between the hotel staff, the kind Scottish people, their hometown travel agency, credit card companies, and the U.S. embassy, they were able to obtain new clothing, passports, money, tickets home, and even a claim check for their car, parked at Boston's Logan Airport.

This is their advice for other travelers:

✓ Get in the habit of thinking through what you would do if you had to leave your hotel room in seconds' time. Put all your essentials — eyeglasses, passport, money, tickets — in a handbag or other small travel bag and *hang it on the doorknob.*

✓ Keep a robe and slippers or a raincoat and shoes easily accessible so that you can grab them on your way out.

✓ Leave with a relative or a friend a list of all your essential numbers: passport number and date, traveler's check numbers, credit card numbers, and your travel agent's phone number. See the Safety Numbers List, page 208.

✓ Most important, *leave the room immediately.*

HOTEL OPTIONS

You can usually book a room the same day in small towns in most countries, especially off season. Exceptions abound, of course: a college town may have a parents' weekend; a local festival or sports event may fill all the vacancies in a small village. The next town will probably have rooms available. In Europe look for a round blue sign with a lowercase "i," indicating an information service.

European hotels often have a variety of room and bath options. The top of the line is the bedroom with an attached bath and toilet. If you ask for a bed and bath you may get a bedroom with a shower stall, with the toilet down the hall, so if you want a toilet in your room you must ask for it. Bathrooms in older European hotels often do not include a toilet. (If you're looking for a toilet, don't be polite and ask for a bathroom — that may be all you get!)

If a hotel has a feature you simply love, such as a nice view from your window or a pleasant courtyard to sit in, take it. That's what good memories are made of, but remember that that's also what eats up your money.

You'll have the best luck if you look for and decide on your hotel in the late morning or early afternoon. Leave your luggage with the concierge or room clerk and you can go out and enjoy yourself for the rest of the day.

If you haven't booked ahead, try to give yourself enough time to find a hotel before you're desperate with fatigue. In looking for a hotel, I make a point of checking out three places before committing to stay. The most visible hotel is usually not the cheapest.

If you arrive in late evening, however, you may also be able to negotiate the price of a room, since the hotel may prefer having the room occupied for a lower price than having the room empty.

In Asia, at major transportation terminals you'll be surrounded by taxi drivers urging you to go with them to one hotel or another. They are paid by the hotel. I've had good luck sizing up drivers who looked decent and honest, and letting them take me to their hotels. Make sure the hotel is where you want to be — downtown, for example, or near the train station.

Budget travelers should look for the friendly neighborhood hotel that caters to locals, not the fancy place that caters to tourists. For instance, in Paris a friend found a clean, respectable hotel in a lovely old part of town for $10 a night — and had several to choose from — simply by walking around and inquiring at neighborhood hotels instead of at obvious tourist places.

Ask what the exact price will be, including tax and service charge, when you accept the room so that you know what to expect on the bill. Have the desk clerk or concierge write down the figure.

Breakfast in continental Europe ("Continental Breakfast") is a cup of coffee with hot milk and a roll with jam and butter. In Great Britain and

Ireland, on the other hand, breakfast is enormous — juice, cereal, eggs, bacon or ham or both, racks of toast, crumpets or scones, jam, marmalade, cakes, and pots of tea.

***Pension complet* and *demi-pension* are especially good deals** in a two-star hotel with a three-star restaurant. The price includes your lodging and food for one day. You'll be tempted to stay forever! *Pension complet* includes a continental breakfast, lunch (often a large one), and dinner. Usually you eat the fixed menu or plate-of-the-day with few or no choices. *Demi-pension* includes a continental breakfast and one other meal, usually dinner. This is a good choice for those who wish to tour or hike during the day but return to the hotel in the evening.

The American Plan means you get a big "American breakfast," lunch, and dinner included in the price of your lodging; the Modified American Plan (MAP) means just breakfast.

A restaurant in the hotel is convenient, but does raise the price. If you're on a budget, look for a hotel without a restaurant and ask the desk clerk or concierge to recommend a nearby eating place.

A Friend Indeed

Your concierge is guardian of your privacy and safety; hailer of taxis; fountain of information about bus routes, good restaurants, theater tickets, reliable doctors, and pharmacies with all-night hours; and, in general, your link to the world you're visiting.

Check with the national tourist office or city tourist office for a lodging reservation service. In Great Britain, for example, you can arrive in a city, go to the office of the National Tourist Board (always conveniently located), and book a room at a local B&B. I've done this even at eleven o'clock at night, although that's risky at the height of the season.

You can book a room ahead of time in the city you expect to reach that evening. Give your estimated time of arrival so that they don't give your room away if you arrive after supper. Then you can travel to your destination in a carefree and leisurely way.

ᴵᴵᴵ **IN THE UNITED STATES** ᴵᴵᴵ
AND CANADA

In the United States, a guide to budget motels, bed-and-breakfast places, or campgrounds will save you a lot of money and time, especially if you're traveling with your family. Plan your route ahead of time, and make your reservations. This is far more reliable than trying to find an inexpensive motel at the end of the day. It also helps you to budget your lodging cost in advance.

To get good hotel rates, try calling the Hotel Reservations Network (see Useful Addresses, page 217), which purchases blocks of hotel rooms and sells them to you at a discount.

YMCAs and YWCAs are safe, clean, and reliable in the United States and Canada, as in cities throughout the world. Many offer family accommodations and have recreational facilities, such as gyms and pools. Canadian Y's are an excellent value. To reserve a room, send the Y a post-card with your expected date of arrival. This may not hold your room under pressure, but it can help.

If you stay at a hotel chain at each stop along your trip, you can make all your reservations at once.

ᴵᴵᴵ **HOSTELS** ᴵᴵᴵ

Hostels are not only for young people. The International Youth Federations now has a card that affords a discount to people over fifty-nine. Get a copy of the *International Youth Hostel Handbook* (different volumes cover different areas of the world) for specific addresses and facilities. Write to the American Youth Hostels (see Useful Addresses) for a membership card.

Hostels are reliable, cheap, clean, safe, and fun. They also have certain rules. You must carry your membership card. Men sleep in one dormitory and women in another (although some hostels have a few rooms for couples or families). The doors may be locked as early as ten o'clock (a few stay open until midnight). There's a maximum number of nights you can stay, and usually you aren't allowed to hang around during the day.

A hostel may serve communal meals or it may have a kitchen, equipped with utensils, for you to use (you're expected to clean up after yourself).

Hostels are ideal for solo travelers — you have other people to talk to and you might meet another single you'd like to travel with. In this country and abroad, you'll meet people from all over the world.

Hostels may not be conveniently located. The original purpose of hostels was to serve people who are roughing it — hiking or bicycling. Thus they're located in scenic areas, not necessarily convenient to the city center.

Arrive when the hostel opens in the afternoon, to assure yourself of a bed. You'll need to have your own towel, soap, and sheet. A sleeping sack is often recommended — just fold a single flat sheet lengthwise and stitch around one short end and the long side.

OTHER ACCOMMODATIONS

Staying in castles is a very special experience — exciting for children, romantic for couples. You'll need reservations; use your guidebook or inquire at a national tourist bureau. You can also choose from farmhouse accommodations, canal boats, abbeys, and private homes.

Why not rent a villa? Especially if you have children, this is a delightful way to visit France, Italy, Portugal, Spain, Malta, or Greece. Friends of mine rented a lovely villa in Spain through At Home Abroad (see Useful Addresses).

Camping is very popular in Europe. Invest in the National Camper Association "carnet," a card that can get you a discount to many camp-grounds throughout the world. Reserve a space ahead of time.

For information on rentals all over the world, read the classified ads in the *International Herald Tribune* or in local foreign papers.

If you're traveling on a budget in South or Central America, be sure to buy a hammock. You'll use it in beach cabañas, on river boats, and even in cheap hotel rooms.

DINING

If you plan to splurge on anything, let it be on food. Whether it's a new fruit in South America or a new wine in France, raw fish at a Japanese *sushi-ya* or fish and chips by a London dock, discovering new foods is one of the great pleasures of and reasons for traveling.

Read up on the cuisine ahead of time, if you'll be in a country where English isn't spoken, so that you won't be totally ignorant of the country's specialities. Purchase a phrase book before you go and study the section on reading menus. The *Berlitz Guide to Latin American Spanish for Travelers,* for example, has a substantial section on menus, with a page devoted to each of a dozen courses — and it makes a few recommendations as well. (Don't worry that a phrase book might make you look like a tourist. Your concern is with having a delicious meal.)

Most guidebooks will also include pointers for negotiating a foreign menu. If you don't want to take the entire book into the restaurant, just clip and staple the relevant section and carry it in your pocket or handbag.

Ask at the city tourist office for information on restaurants. Also use your guidebook, and ask your concierge or hotel desk clerk for recommendations.

Ask for your waiter's recommendation. And be adventurous! Don't order the same dish everywhere you go — try something new.

In many parts of the world the midday meal constitutes the main meal of the day, after a skimpy continental breakfast. In Great Britain and Ireland, though, both breakfast and the midday meal tend to be hearty, especially in rural areas, followed by a light "tea" at suppertime and another "tea" (usually sweet breads and cakes) just before bed.

Carry picnic supplies with you, if you're driving. Wash up your dishes at a rest area if your picnic site has no running water. Have with you a couple of dish towels, a small cutting board, a good knife, can and bottle openers, a cup for each person, a thermos, a roll of plastic bags, and a roll of paper towels. Paper products are hard to find outside the United States and Canada; invest in a set of plates and flatware, and some sort of container to keep everything in. It goes without saying that you should take with you, when you leave, any trash your picnic generates.

Keeping Restaurants within Your Means

- Read the menu before you sit down (it's usually posted, in this country, Europe, and Asia).

- Look for smorgasbords, buffets, salad bars, and other "all-you-can-eat" situations, and make this the big meal of the day.

- Choose the special of the day.

- Order a complete dinner, not individual items à la carte.

- When in Europe, Canada, and the United States, patronize Asian restaurants.

- For health as well as economy, eat vegetarian.

In many parts of the world, shops and offices close down for lunch from noon until about two o'clock. Restaurants often cater to this by serving an inexpensive full meal. For those on a budget, this is the time to eat the big meal of the day.

Many restaurants also have a fixed meal — one or two choices of appetizer, a salad, main course, one or two choices of dessert — which might in France be called *Le Menu* or *Le Plat du Jour* (the menu in France is *la carte,* which can be confusing!). This is always the best deal for the money, and the freshest food.

Break the three-main-meals-a-day habit, and you'll save money. Have a light lunch or a light supper.

⌡⌡ AT THE TABLE ⌡⌡

In many parts of the world, silverware is not a part of the mealtime scene. Chopsticks, used throughout East Asia, don't take long to master if you keep at it and don't get embarrassed by your first fumblings.

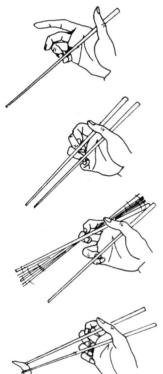

A. *Hold one chopstick in the U-shaped area between thumb and index finger, and rest the lower end on the top of your ring finger.*

B. *Hold the other chopstick with thumb, index finger, and middle finger, as if it were a pencil.*

C. *Manipulate upper chopstick, using thumb as pivot.*

D. *Enjoy!*

Eating with one's fingers, as is done throughout South Asia, is traumatic for the Western visitor. In restaurants, forks and spoons will be provided, but private homes usually lack them. I traveled through India using a mess kit fork and spoon, until my husband and I sat down to a meal in a lovely home among gracious friends. They were eating with their fingers, and I couldn't bring myself to pull out the utensils. Remember to eat with your right hand as Asians do (although Asians have come to accept Western quirks). They customarily use the left hand for all unsanitary tasks and the right hand for eating. You may not be given a napkin, but you'll probably be given a finger bowl.

In Europe, people tend to hold their fork in their left hand and their knife in the right, to eliminate the awkwardness of switching utensils back and forth. This is an easy and graceful habit to pick up.

Eat yogurt to cool your palate after a meal that's highly spiced with chili pepper or hot curries. Or do what the Mexicans do — eat *more* hot food.

Dining in France

There are special traditions associated with dining out in France. Eating fine French food in a good restaurant should not be missed, and I recommend it as a very special occasion to splurge, even when traveling with children.

- Remember that you must call a good restaurant for a reservation. Once you have a reservation, however, you have the table all night and you can concentrate totally on your meal and your companions.
- Restaurants in France tend to open later for dinner — half-past seven or so. Service can be leisurely. After dessert, you're expected to linger over coffee. If you don't ask for your bill ("L'addition, s'il vous plaît!") with your coffee, you may have a long wait.
- When ordering, ask your waiter's recommendation. More and more waiters in Parisian restaurants understand English. You should try speaking in French, as well; I've never experienced the surliness with which French waiters supposedly greet American French.
- Learn the French words for animal body parts. Feet, blood sausage, brains, and many other organs are considered delicacies in France.
- Tips are included in the bill (but not in the price on the menu) in most of France. Most menus or bills say "Service Compris," which means that the management has added in 15 percent, so you need not tip. If you've received extraordinary service, however, you may leave a "pour boire" — a little something for a drink.
- Where service isn't included, a 15 percent tip is standard.

⏐⏐⏐⏐12⏐⏐⏐⏐

ENJOYING YOURSELF

I suspect you don't need much advice on how to enjoy yourself while traveling, but here are a few suggestions that have helped me in the past.

Get up at or before dawn. Seeing how the day begins, whether by hearing the roosters crow in the West Indies or observing the bicycle rush hour in Beijing, lets you *in* to an unfamiliar place. I have an indelible memory of the beautiful city of Quito, Ecuador, slowly coming to life before dawn as market vendors streamed in from the villages to set up their booths, carrying huge bundles of fruits and vegetables on their backs or on donkeys. Certain places are truly sublime at dawn — the Grand Canyon, for example, or the Taj Mahal — and you probably won't be sharing them with other tourists!

Walk. It's the single best mode of transportation. Whether you're in San Francisco or the Himalayas, walking will give you a flavor of the place you can't get enclosed in a vehicle. It helps you to know where you are — and it's good for you besides.

Take different forms of transportation. You can ride a camel to see the Pyramids, take a skiing tour through Norway, or ride horseback through Outer Mongolia. Ask your travel agent. In particular, take boats. You can float through the canals of Amsterdam, Bangkok, and, of course, Venice. You can rent canal boats in France or England. You can take steamers up the Rhine or the Danube past romantic castles, take the Circle Tour of New York City, or take swan boats in Boston's Public Garden. Eurailpass covers ferries between many European countries; it will cover most of the cost of the boat from Corfu, Greece, across the Adriatic to Brindisi, Italy.

Forget your prejudices against museums. The small museum at the Grand Canyon, the Whaling Museum on Nantucket Island, the museum at Omaha Beach in Normandy — these are places children will never forget.

Find out what events are taking place while you're visiting. Every area has its own specialty that's featured in a festival. There are festivals celebrating corn and rhubarb in South Dakota, maple syrup in Vermont, zucchini in New Hampshire, tobacco in Kentucky, and oysters in Louisiana.

Don't forget town, county, and state fairs, which take place in the summer and fall. County fairs are my favorite — large enough to be exciting, but not too sophisticated. I recommend the Dutchess County Fair in Rhinebeck, New York, for wonderful food and atmosphere.

Talk to people, in their own language, if possible.

If you find you constantly meet the same Americans over and over, it means you probably have the same guidebook. Often Americans are embarrassed at seeing others of their own nationality. Don't be. Instead, make friends with the people you keep running into. You and they evidently have the same tastes and the same traveling style, and probably have a great deal more in common. You'll get the most useful tips of all from your fellow travelers.

Be sensitive to local customs. Honor all religious prescripts — you must slip out of your shoes to enter a Muslim, Hindu, Sikh, or Buddhist shrine, and you must put on a hat to enter certain churches. Women are not supposed to sit next to Buddhist monks (on public transportation, for example). You must rely on a guidebook for this kind of specific information.

Follow your instincts. A friend describes driving through France with her husband. They had planned the basic route and the towns they wanted to visit, but when they spotted a small sign saying "Roquefort" they were intrigued and made a spontaneous detour. They discovered a

Above All, Be Adventurous

Remember that the great travel experiences belong to those who are ready for them. My husband and I were once on an ancient public bus, toiling up the dizzying heights of the Himalayas. My fear of heights was so strong that I had my eyes closed most of the time. My husband, meanwhile, was gazing out over spectacular vistas, seeing from an eagle's perspective the endless mountain ranges stretching out. His wise suggestion to me was to feel the fear, but to keep looking anyway — not to miss one of the greatest sights a human being could see. Be cautious, be careful, but don't let that interfere with enjoying the magnificent adventure of travel.

lovely village, the source of the famous cheese, and some fascinating caves to explore as well. Remember that the best part of travel is discovering things for yourself.

Enhance your enjoyment of a package tour by advance preparation — knowing exactly where the tour takes you and reading up on the background of the places. Collect addresses of people you can drop in on. Make the most of your free time.

MEETING PEOPLE

The warmest memories of your trip will undoubtedly involve the new friends you've made. Whether natives or tourists like yourself, they make your trip more special and meaningful, and some may become lifelong friends.

Some countries are easier for meeting people than others. Where tourists are rarely seen, you'll frequently find yourself surrounded by interested natives, and you'll often be invited for tea and a chat. In other countries, people might be reluctant to invade your privacy. In particular, men tend to have difficulty meeting local women abroad.

Despite the stereotype of the "ugly American," most people do in fact want to meet Americans. A friend who knows and loves France reports that older French people still remember and honor Americans who served in the Second World War. If you're a veteran, or your parents or grandparents were veterans, you'll be warmly received. Be sure to let the local people know if you're on a pilgrimage back to towns where you stayed or fought during the war. There are a number of war memorials and museums honoring those who served.

Seek out friends of friends. First and foremost, before you leave home, gather from your friends the addresses of *their* friends living abroad. This is the best way to enter into the life of the country you're visiting, to experience the way people live — and to sample home cooking! You can write a note in advance of your trip, or have your American friends do so, or you can drop a line when you're in the vicinity. Offer to bring a present or photographs from your American friends. The people you visit may then send you to their friends, until you have a network of acquaintances around the country.

Bring little gifts of your own for the people listed in your address book. Easy-to-carry but much-appreciated presents include T-shirts, lighters, novel pens, little flashlights, baseball caps, and scarves. Blue jeans and denim jackets take up more room in your suitcase but are

What Would You Do If...

You're nineteen years old, on your first trip abroad. You've been traveling for three days, you can't shake the jet lag, you haven't met anyone, and you can't speak the language. You've got three more weeks to go. How will you get through this?

Be sure to have a calling card. Find a pay phone to call home or a friend. Have a good chat. Then treat yourself to a good meal and go to bed early. Write your feelings in a journal. Next day, shake off the blues by going to a place where you'll be with local children — a puppet show, a zoo, a children's museum.

greatly appreciated by teenagers. Sweatshirts with sports insignia are also a huge success. Avoid giving candy, especially in countries where dental care is hard to obtain.

For recreation, do as the locals do. Go to football games, flea markets, fairs, and festivals. In Northern Europe, where the locals tend to respect your privacy, the best place by far to meet people is in the local pub. Most pubs attract both sexes and all ages, and the atmosphere is warm and congenial. Your new acquaintances will buy you drinks; etiquette demands that you "stand a round" yourself. If you don't drink, just substitute a soft drink.

Take public transportation. Traveling in a rented car can be isolating. Instead, try local buses — always a memorable experience. Trains are classic places to meet people. Conversations are struck up effortlessly in train compartments and may result in exchanged addresses and lifelong friendships.

A picture can lead to a thousand words. When you take photographs of a local, you might offer or be asked to send a copy to your subject. This can lead to a long-term correspondence.

Attend religious services. You'll be surrounded by people at the end of the service. Remember that there are customs governing dress in churches, temples, and synagogues.

To meet fellow travelers, try "American" places. The American Express office or the American embassy — wherever you receive your mail — is a natural place.

LANGUAGE

Not only will you get around better if you try to speak the language, but you'll also make more friends. People everywhere appreciate your effort to communicate on their terms, and many deeply resent the American who assumes everyone speaks English.

Learning a language is easiest when you're immersed in it, surrounded by native speakers. You'll have exact pronunciations to imitate, and you'll tune in to the flowing rhythms of speech. Even if you could never pass French 101, you'll find yourself picking up the language now.

Purchase an instructional language cassette a few months before departure. Play it regularly to get the sound of the language in your ears. Keep it on while you pack your suitcase.

Dictionaries and phrase books can help. Pick up a small paperback dictionary of the language and a pocket phrase book. Phrase books are useful for specific situations, but a dictionary will help you really learn the language.

Don't be embarrassed. Key to learning a language, as with many skills, is a lack of embarrassment. You can't learn a new language without making mistakes. If the fear of erring keeps you from practicing, then you'll never be able to speak fluently.

Learn three or four related words at once, which is just as easy as learning one. Choose a few words that might be used together — "to walk," "to look for," "to see." (See the box below for other suggestions.) If you'll be off the beaten path, it's more crucial to have a smattering of the language. If you visit in a country with an alphabet different from ours, become as familiar as possible with the letters so that at the very least, you can make out the road signs.

Pay attention to proprieties. Note that in many countries there's both an informal and a formal way of saying "you." To learn when each form is appropriate takes time, and comes as you get to know the particular culture. In French, for example, the formal *vous* is expected when you first meet people. When you hear them start using *tu* in addressing you, then you may do the same. Many people older than sixty, however, are more formal, and will continue to use the *vous* form even after you've come to know them quite well. Don't feel insulted — they may use the *tu* form only with their immediate families. If you're young, on the other hand, other young people may never use the *vous* form with you, just as it's more likely that you'll be addressed by a Spanish contemporary as *tu* instead of *usted,* even when you first meet. Take your lead from the people you're with, but if in doubt always use the polite form.

Consider attending language classes or hiring a tutor if you'll be in one country for a while. The formal instruction will help make sense of the language you hear all around you. With a tutor the price will vary according to his or her age and experience. You don't necessarily need an expert teacher, just a native speaker. Your tutor may become an important resource for you. A man who tutored my husband and me in Hindi in India ended up becoming a good friend, taking us to weddings, political rallies, and family occasions, and even teaching us to cook Indian style.

Electronic translators are another option. Refer to Useful Addresses, page 217, for where you can purchase electronic translators of different types.

Words to Learn Ahead of Time

- Become familiar with the personal pronouns (you, I, etc.) in their different forms.

- Learn the verb "to be" and put it together with the different personal pronouns (I am, you are, etc.). Then do the same thing with the verbs "to go" and "to have." Notice what it sounds like when these three very useful verbs are spoken on your instructional cassette. You'll see that by following these with different verbs you'll be able to say a great deal.

- Learn how to say "Where is . . . ?"

- Learn the polite words — hello, please, thank you, excuse me, and goodbye, as well as "I am an American," "I don't understand," and "Do you speak English?"

- Learn emergency words: "I need a doctor!"; "Help!"; and "Where is the toilet?"

- Try to learn at least five new words a day.

13

SHOPPING

My grandmother was a passionate world traveler. Her return from a place like Burma was always a wonderful event, partly because she always sat down with her grandchildren and had us guess what she had brought each of us. The presents were always tiny animals — a glass horse, a wooden tiger, a papier-mâché elephant — small enough to fit in one's hand. We were enchanted by the foreignness of the gifts. Not only have we treasured them ever since, but we also now believe they were the perfect type of present to bring back from a foreign place — tiny, inexpensive, and delightful.

Keep to a minimum the number of expensive gifts you buy. It's impossible to bring gifts for everyone you'd like to. Inexpensive items could include a tape or compact disc; foodstuffs, such as mustard, jams, chocolates, or chutney; a silk scarf from Asia or a tartan scarf from Scotland; a cookbook; color slides; inexpensive handmade jewelry; or a little book of postcards.

Research the specialties of the place before you leave on your trip. Then check out the prices of the same items in this country. For example, can you purchase a Belleek tea service cheaper through a catalog, in an American gift shop, in an Irish or British gift shop, or at the factory shop in Northern Ireland? Travelers often complain that they thought they found a great deal while on a trip, only to come home and find the same item selling for less here.

Avoid impulse buying. Have a general idea of what you want to purchase, in order to limit impulse buying. Make a list, based on books about the place you are visiting, guidebooks, newspaper travel sections, and information from tourist offices. Make another list of the people for whom you want to buy gifts, and how much you intend to spend. Keep this in a little notebook to take shopping. Know people's measurements, and bring along a measuring tape, since sizes will be different abroad.

Ask around when you reach your destination. Inquire at the tourist office about where the best deals may be. Are there any craft fairs? What about street markets? Are there seasonal sales, such as post-Christmas sales in January? Talk to other tourists and, even more importantly, to locals, to learn about any special shops, areas, good deals, or interesting items they've discovered.

Visit a museum before you buy craft items. To learn about the special features of handicrafts you may want to buy, go to a museum. This might help you to distinguish treasures from junk and will place the items in a historical and artistic context.

Give yourself time. If you have a few days to shop, spend the first one simply wandering — window-shopping and browsing. Bring along your notebook to record any useful information: prices, store names, differences in quality. On your second day, you can simply go directly to the place with the best deal and make your purchase with confidence.

Keep good records. When you *do* buy something, jot down the date, the amount in foreign currency, and what you paid in U.S. dollars. Be sure to save the receipt, because you may need to show it when you come through customs. Even in this country, it's useful to keep a record of the date purchased and the price.

Visit grocery stores. Be sure to shop in a grocery store in a foreign country. Whether it's a French supermarket or an Asian bazaar, you'll enjoy the contrast of the exotic and the familiar. Bring along a net or plastic bag. In many parts of the world grocery bags don't exist, and it's customary to bring your own.

Remember how credit card charges get billed abroad. Paying by credit card means that you'll be billed at the exchange rate in effect on the day the charge clears in the United States, not the rate on the day you made the purchase. Thus you cannot predict exactly how much you'll be paying, or whether it'll be more or less.

Be aware of duty charges. The booklet *Know Before You Go,* available from the U.S. Customs Service (see Useful Addresses, page 217), lists duty charges for you. The duty may be so small that it's worth buying certain articles even if you have to pay duty on them.

Mailing an item may have a hidden cost. A $400 per person duty-free allowance applies only to things you carry home. Except for gifts valued under $50, anything you mail home will be subject to duty. (See Chapter 16, "Coming Home.") On the other hand, shipping things home, although costly, will get your things from the shop right to your door.

Never assume "duty-free" means "best buy." Duty-free shops may not be as cheap as stores in the United States, especially for spirits. Again, know your prices.

ⅲ **V-A T** ⅲ

In most countries you must pay a Value Added Tax (the VAT has different names in different countries), a sales tax that residents of the country must also pay. You can get reimbursed for it (as much as 30 percent of the cost of an item) if you obtain a special form from the merchant. Some shops require that you spend a certain minimum before they will reimburse you. When you leave the country, give the form to a customs officer, who will sign it and send it to the Customs Office. It is then sent to your merchant, who, instead of paying that tax to the government, sends it to you.

The rationale behind this system is that although the residents of the country are taxed, the government wants to encourage *your* business. Yet if you didn't have to pay the VAT at all, or if you were reimbursed on the spot, you might turn around and sell the item to a resident in order to make a profit for yourself.

Keep your VAT forms organized. In order to be reimbursed, you must be certain that your shop will follow through and that you have the form signed when you leave the country. Crossing the borders of some countries involves so little formality that you could easily forget to turn in the form. If this happens, try sending the form, signed by the U.S. Customs Office, to the customs service of the country you were visiting.

ⅢⅡ B A R G A I N I N G ⅢⅡ

Bargaining has been part of buying and selling for thousands of years. You're at a disadvantage when bargaining with a shrewd, seasoned negotiator, because our culture doesn't allow us to sharpen our wits at this activity. If the seller agrees with our offer, then we think we must have started bargaining too high; yet we're reluctant to haggle too aggressively for fear of offending.

In many developing countries, if you don't haggle over the price of local crafts or produce, and simply pay the first price asked, you may be driving up the price of goods for locals and subsequent tourists.

No "right price" exists, especially for craft items. The right price is what both sides agree to — it varies according to the context. Again, be familiar with the prices of comparable items back home.

Shop around, especially at a craft market, where many different vendors sell similar items. Check what various sellers are asking. When you find a big price discrepancy, you can ask, "Why is this more expensive here than from that man over there?" Perhaps the quality differs, and the vendor will educate you. Or perhaps your question will be taken as a bargaining ploy, and the original price may come down.

Don't worry about demanding too low a price. If the seller cannot accept the price, he or she will not. And don't worry about a price difference that might amount to a few U.S. cents. If you like the item, purchase it at a medium price and everyone will be satisfied.

Put energy into your bargaining. Merchants seem to love a vigorous negotiation, and may enjoy themselves enough to give you a good price.

Children are often good bargainers. They seem to have the correct combination of passion and indifference.

Shop both early and late in the day. The best purchases are often made in the early morning, when the vendor is just setting up, and at dusk, when he or she is packing everything away. Some vendors are superstitious and like to encourage a first sale of the day to get the morning started well. Others try to make a final sale before packing up, so that they have less to take home.

Know which items are duty exempt. Certain goods from certain countries — usually the products of cottage industries that don't compete with our economy, such as Mexican ceramics — are exempted from duty. This is called the Generalized System of Preferences. Write to U.S. Customs for a booklet called *GSP and the International Traveler* (see Useful Addresses).

Bartering

In some parts of the world you'll be able to barter. In Kenya, for example, you can barter for jewelry or for bold printed cottons. Good things to bring along for this are T-shirts, pens, digital watches, baseball caps, socks, scarves, and sunglasses.

14

PHOTOGRAPHY

There are many reasons *not* to take a camera along on a trip. It's cumbersome, fragile, and a constant security headache. Being overly concerned with videos or photographs can interfere with your enjoyment. While you're busy loading the camera and snapping away, you miss seeing things with your own eyes. Then if the pictures don't come out, you've lost everything.

Yet you want visual records of your trip. Here's a time when you have to weigh which is more important to you — the actual experience of the trip, or the memory of it.

Consider taking along a disposable or "Instamatic"-type camera — one that's inexpensive, light, small, simple, and not too precious to lose. It should have a built-in flash. The camera's limitations will keep you from looking at your trip through a lens. Instead, you'll merely be keeping records of friends' faces, memorable events, places, and celebrations. And if the camera is lost or stolen you won't be devastated — your biggest loss will be the roll of pictures inside it.

Or you can take an inexpensive Polaroid instant camera. Both camera and film are bulky and technically limited, but you'll be able to delight your models with gifts of instant pictures. Partway through your trip, when your camera gets too heavy, you can give it to a new acquaintance.

Better cameras have significant drawbacks. That said, let's discuss more-expensive equipment. Depending on your expertise, you may want to take a small, fully automatic single-lens reflex camera with a built-in flash; a simple, basic, 35-millimeter camera; or a video camera. If you do decide to take an expensive camera, be prepared to protect it from loss, theft, and damage throughout your trip. If your camera is foreign made, register it with U.S. Customs before you leave this country. Otherwise, you may be charged duty on it when you return. If you cannot register it, take along the sales receipt.

Make sure you're absolutely familiar with your camera before your trip, whatever kind you bring. Shoot at least five rolls of film and have them developed before you go so that you know the camera and how it performs under various conditions of light, focus, film speed, flash, and so on. While traveling you probably won't be developing film (processing film abroad tends to be much more expensive and of much poorer quality than here in the United States), so you won't receive the vital feedback of seeing your photos. Know what kind of effects you can produce with your camera in different situations — action shots, portraits, landscapes. Learn how quickly you can whip it out and have it focused for that once-in-a-lifetime shot.

ᛁᛁᛁ L-E N S-E S ᛁᛁᛁ

When deciding what lenses to take, ask yourself what kind of pictures you'll be taking. Wildlife and landscape photography demands a different lens than people and action shots do.

A zoom lens offers versatility, but you lose lens speed, ease of focus, and sharpness, and the lens is heavy and bulky besides. Carrying multiple lenses, on the other hand, can cost you precious minutes getting the right one on for the shot. If you solve this problem the way news photographers do — with several cameras around your neck — have you ever encumbered yourself!

I recommend that you carry just a fast normal lens. If you take a second lens, it could be a zoom (35 to 105 millimeter).

Use a haze filter to protect your lens.

⌇⌇⌇ FILM AND BATTERIES ⌇⌇⌇

Buy film before leaving home. Make a reasonable estimate of how much film you'll need for the trip. Then double it. New sights and surroundings will arouse your photographic urges. The film you buy in advance will be of excellent quality and probably cheaper than that available in most other countries.

Take color slide film if you have access to a slide projector at home. You can then have just the best shots made into prints.

Carry extra batteries. In addition to the set of batteries in your camera, take a set for every two weeks you'll be gone. Batteries may cost more than twice as much in a foreign country as in the United States.

Buying film abroad can be expensive and risky. When you buy film in some less-developed countries you have to be alert. Kodak and Ilford can cost more than $10 per roll. If you decide you want to test the local brand of film, you should try to have a roll developed to determine its quality. If you run out of film and want to purchase a familiar kind, never let a shopkeeper sell you name-brand film and load it in your camera before you've made sure that the seal is intact. This once happened to me, just outside the gate of the Taj Mahal, when I was desperate for film. I found out later that the film I purchased was not in fact Kodak, but some other type, attached to a reel with a piece of adhesive tape, rolled up, and placed in a Kodak box. I was lucky that the film hadn't been exposed already.

Useful Photography Supplies
■ Lens tissue
■ Extra batteries
■ Carrying case and strap
■ Protective bag for film
■ Extra lens cover
■ Haze filter
■ Small notebook for recording photos

ᴵᴵᴵ TAKING PICTURES ᴵᴵᴵ

Shoot early in the day and late in the afternoon. The most important photography tip may be to get up early, before dawn if possible. You can watch a place come slowly to life, and the light often has an especially evocative quality. The other best time to take pictures, I feel, is in the "champagne" light of late afternoon.

Protect your equipment. For example, if you'll be shooting on a beach or in the desert, where the wind can whip sand into the cracks of your camera, make sure you carry it in a case and that you have a protective haze filter over the lens.

Beware of unusual photography conditions. For example, snow and sand can be very bright and may throw off a camera's automatic setting. Read your camera manual to find out how best to deal with this. When in tricky situations — or when taking the shot of your lifetime — bracket your exposures: take three of the same shot at different settings.

Put people in your pictures. A common mistake travelers make is to dutifully photograph monument after monument. This can make for very boring viewing later. Include people in your pictures — either locals or your own group.

Take pictures of the friends you make! Of all your photos, these will be the ones you cherish most.

People provide scale. If you take a picture of something enormous or something tiny, incorporate a person or part of a person for scale. And always get close enough so that your subject fills the frame.

Get photos of the local people, in farmer's markets, at sports events, at festivals, and so on, even though you may not find it easy to photograph people discreetly. Modest women or elderly people may turn away in embarrassment or disapproval; children may overreact and pester you to take more pictures.

Obey proscriptions! Some ethnic groups prohibit photography. The Hopi Indians of Arizona, for example, will confiscate cameras of offending tourists.

Try "shooting from the hip" — holding your camera waist high. Practice before you go.

Memories beat photos. Every photographer mourns a missed picture, whether of a shy smile creasing a weathered face or of an elephant crossing a river at dawn. Remember, though, that a lost picture indelibly engraved in your memory is even better than if you had caught it on film.

Don't expect good pictures while flying. If you shoot from an airplane window, try to avoid sitting where the wing will dominate your photo (although a slice of it can add some drama). Place your lens right against the window so that your picture won't pick up the scratches on the glass. The corners and edges of an airplane window are very distorted, so try to keep your camera directed out the middle. To get good shots from a plane window, you'll have to be ready just after the plane takes off. Within two minutes you'll be too high to make anything out.

Pay to Snap

The Taos Pueblo in New Mexico allows picture-taking but charges a per-camera fee. In other places, posing for tourists has become a real industry. Whether or not to tip your model has to be dealt with in context. I've never actually done this, preferring to offer to send the person a picture (and then following through!). But offering a coin may be the only way to get the exact photo you want. Be aware, though, that posing for pictures may be a profitable business for your subject.

VIDEOTAPING

A fact of travel (and life) is that you spend more time remembering things than you do experiencing them. This is why many inexperienced travelers spend an entire trip with a video camera clamped to their faces, in order to have high-quality images to enhance their memories. In a sense, they're saving the pleasure to enjoy at a later time. But they've cheated themselves of truly experiencing and enjoying the trip in the present tense — the broad spectrum of sounds, smells, and other sensations, and their feelings about what they're perceiving. Many videographers become obsessed with capturing every detail (I know: I've done it).

If you have small children, it's tempting to record their trip as it unfolds, to help them remember it. But again, this removes you from experiencing it with them. One good tip is to film a few interviews with the children in a scenic or otherwise memorable spot.

Security

Although security equipment at U.S. and European airports won't harm your film, in other countries you may have to protect it to be sure you won't lose every shot you took. Hand your film and your loaded camera to the security guard for a manual inspection.

You have to strike a balance. It's important to experience the trip fully. Videotapes are never a match for your memories; they're really best to show to other people, once. Keeping a journal is a better way to preserve the moment. And make time, when you return, to reminisce with your companions or reflect on your own about your experiences.

ᴵᴵᴵ DEVELOPING ᴵᴵᴵ

When traveling in the United States, you can take along a number of pre-paid envelopes from a mail-order film developing house. Send back the film as you shoot it, and your prints or slides will be waiting for you when you arrive home.

If mailing film from abroad, take precautions. Be sure to send it air mail. Mark the package "FILM" so that it will (hopefully) not be x-rayed. Traveler's Checklist (see Useful Addresses, page 217) carries a handy film shield that can protect up to twenty-two rolls of 35-mm film or a loaded camera from airport X rays.

Heat kills film. Besides X rays, nothing is more damaging to film than high temperatures. Don't leave film or your camera in a closed, hot car or the trunk.

Cold can also harm film. Extreme cold can also adversely affect film, making it brittle and even causing cracks or breaks. Wrap film you're about to use in something woolen, or put a roll or two in your pockets for a short time, to keep it warm, pliable, and manageable.

|||15|||
SAFETY AND SECURITY

Once I was walking through an Old Delhi market when a crowd of women beggars approached me, thrusting out their hands and demanding money. As I continued on, the women became more aggressive. I turned and spoke sharply to them, and the next moment they were gone.

I felt quite proud of myself until I realized that the closed zipper on my shoulder bag had split open. My wallet had vanished along with the band of women, into one of the thousands of alleys that thread that teeming city. Luckily, the experience served only as an inexpensive warning. The wallet contained about $5 in rupees. Still safely in the bag was a camera worth $200.

Take very seriously the possibility of being ripped off on your travels, and try to manage things so that whatever you lose is not a great loss, neither important nor valuable.

Don't travel with precious possessions. Leave valuable or irreplaceable items, such as jewelry, priceless documents, and furs, at home in your safe-deposit box.

Protect your true essentials — passport, tickets, traveler's checks, credit cards — on your person, preferably in a zippered inside pocket or under your clothes in a money belt or pouch.

Consider everything else to be replaceable, including your camera. To minimize your worry, bring an inexpensive or disposable camera or insure it before your trip. (See Chapter 14, "Photography.")

Paranoia about being robbed can poison your whole trip. Having protected yourself, you can enjoy a relatively carefree attitude — and you won't have to end your trip if your luggage is stolen.

Be discreet. When you visit a poor country, remember that your very presence betokens a degree of wealth that is inconceivable to the people you meet. If you thoughtlessly flaunt money, you could be said to deserve to be ripped off.

Don't be blasé about personal safety. Although theft is more common in other countries than in the United States, assault and rape are much rarer there than here. Many women travelers report feeling much safer at night in Paris, for example, than in New York. If you have doubts about entering a tense area, ask the United States embassy or consulate. Follow their advice!

ᴵⁱˡ MONEY ᴵⁱˡ

Keep your valuables concealed if you're going to be in crowded places. Thieves often work crowd scenes — thronged outdoor events, crowded bus stations and airports. Some thieves specialize in robbing tourists.

Where not to carry money: hip pocket and dangling bags. The two most vulnerable places to keep your money are your back hip pocket and a dangling handbag. The inside breast pocket of a jacket is safer than a hip pocket, if it has a zipper or Velcro tab to seal it. If you carry a handbag or pouch, place the strap over your head as well as your shoulder, and then put your jacket on over the bag. Before your trip, make sure that the zipper, clasp, and straps of your handbag or shoulder bag are rugged and strong. Check them periodically during your travels, and have them repaired if necessary. Remember that an overstuffed bag is likely to burst.

Don't carry excess cash. When you go out at night, especially in a rough neighborhood or red-light district, don't take with you more money than you can afford to lose. Leave the rest in the hotel safe or carefully hidden in your room.

Divide your cash. One friend recommends a double-wallet system. Keep only a small amount of cash in a wallet in the inside breast pocket, and keep the rest of the money in a money belt under your clothes.

Wrap your wallet with rubber bands to make it harder to remove from your pocket without detection.

||| LUGGAGE |||

Secure your luggage before you sleep. If you have to sleep while taking a long journey by train or bus, loop your luggage straps around your arm or leg, or tie your bags to you.

Keep your luggage with you at all times in transportation terminals (unless you can check it). Carry it with you even into a stall in a rest room. Never rely on a nearby stranger to watch your bags.

Pay attention during security checks. One of the times when you are most vulnerable to theft is when you pass through security, because your belongings are momentarily separated from you. Be sure to keep an eye, in particular, on your laptop computer.

Count your bags every time you get off a train or plane or out of a taxi.

When you take a taxi, notice the driver. This is a tip learned through hard experience. If his cab carries his identification, focus on the driver's name; otherwise, notice his looks, the color and type of the vehicle, and so on. I've been known to leave things in taxicabs, but have had 100 percent success in getting them back by piecing together memories of the driver and returning to the taxi stand where I caught the cab. Even though cab drivers may sometimes seem unethical in charging exorbitant rates, they're likely to be honest regarding lost property.

Do not leave valuables in your car, particularly if they're visible, even if the car is locked.

Always watch as a customs official examines your belongings. I once had a recorder lifted by a customs official on the Peru-Bolivia border — an item that never should have been in the luggage atop the bus! Favorite things should stay right next to you.

ⅢⅠ **DOCUMENTS** Ⅲ

Make a safety list before leaving on your trip (see the Safety Numbers List, page 208). This should include a list of traveler's check numbers, emergency refund phone numbers, passport number and date of issue, credit card numbers, airplane ticket numbers, and your itinerary. Make two copies, leave one at home with a friend or house sitter, and bring one with you in your suitcase.

Memorize or copy key passport data. Memorize your passport number and its date and city of issue. Many travelers photocopy the first four pages of their passport and keep the copy in a safe place. It serves as a record of the passport number and other details and will prove invaluable if you require a temporary passport in a foreign country. Be sure to pack a half-dozen extra passport photos (ask for extras when you get the picture taken).

Treat your passport like gold. U.S. passports are worth a lot of money on the black market. Don't give yours to anyone who doesn't have a good reason to see it. Don't use it as collateral for anything. In some areas, however, you may be asked to leave your passport overnight with the hotel management. Ask the desk clerk to write out a receipt for it.

Register your passport if you visit a country that has been in the news recently for any of a number of reasons — natural disaster, transportation accident, change of governments, civil war, terrorism. Register your passport and itinerary with the nearest United States embassy or consulate. You may not be in any actual danger or feel any threat, but your people back home will rest easier if there's a record of your whereabouts.

⑴⑴ HOTEL SAFETY ⑴⑴

Mark your hotel on your map, so that if you get lost and can't speak the language you can point it out to a taxi driver or police officer.

Hotel rooms between the third and sixth floor are safest — high enough to prevent entry from ground level, yet not so high that they can't be reached by fire equipment. Next safest would be a room on the top floor, for access to the roof.

Ask immediately to move if you feel your room is in an unsafe part of the hotel (poor lighting, far from elevator, near back stairway).

Locate the nearest fire exit when you take a room. Look on the back of the door for emergency evacuation procedures posted there by the hotel. Don't just read emergency instructions, rehearse them. Go out into the hall and see where the exit is — count the number of doors from your room to the nearest staircase. In the event of a fire the halls can become engulfed with smoke so thick that you have to crawl along the floor in

What Would You Do If...

You are asleep in your hotel room when suddenly there is a loud pounding on the door. The hotel is on fire and you must leave immediately.

■ *Do not stop to gather your possessions. Leave the room immediately.*

■ *If you have placed your essentials (glasses, money, passport) in your purse or other small bag and hung this on the doorknob, you won't lose any time in taking these valuable items out with you.*

■ *If your possessions are lost in such a disaster, contact your travel agent and your traveler's check and credit card companies. If you are in a foreign country, contact the U.S. embassy or consulate for assistance.*

order to breathe. You may not be able to find the stairs unless you've planned your route. Remember to keep essentials in a handbag or small travel bag and hang this over the doorknob, in case you have to make a rapid exit. (See Chapter 10, "Lodging.")

Check the locks. Make sure that you can lock your room's doors and windows.

Avoid having to fumble for the key. When returning to your room, have your key in your hand before getting on the hotel elevator.

A Few General Safety Tips

- Carry a flashlight in your pocket or purse.

- Make a point of learning how to use the local pay telephone. Often this will require a calling card. In some areas, though, you'll need change. When using some phone systems you don't deposit coins until your party answers; otherwise, you lose your money. Save your change so that you always have the correct coins with you for a phone call.

- Before swimming at an unfamiliar beach, take the time to observe the surf. Are other people swimming? Are they at about your level of competence? Is there a lifeguard on duty? Are there flags or other signs indicating areas that are out of bounds? Don't swim by yourself at an unfamiliar beach unless you've found a sheltered cove where the waves are gentle. (I've found that even so popular a beach as Copacabana in Rio de Janeiro is not for any but the strongest swimmers. A friend and I swam there and felt lucky to emerge alive, pulled out by some young men. My friend's bathing suit was swept off. We realized afterwards that no one else was swimming; it was a sunbathing beach.)

- If you're lucky enough to see wildlife from your car or tour bus, whether bears in Yellowstone Park or tigers in India, view them from the safety of your car. Do not get out to take a picture of a dangerous animal.

Know who's at your door before you open it. If a hotel employee knocks, ask that he or she slide a hotel ID or a room service receipt under the door.

Consider purchasing a small traveling security system, such as the one available through Traveler's Checklist (see Useful Addresses, page 217). This small item, about the size of a transistor radio, combines a burglar alarm, a smoke alarm, an alarm clock, and a powerful flashlight, all in one.

▐▐▌ HANDLING AN EMERGENCY ▐▐▌

When abroad it is essential to have your passport with you at all times. If you get into trouble (an accident in which you were at fault, for example) and don't have your identification, you may be treated like a criminal.

The Overseas Citizens' Emergency Center will help with any complicated medical, financial, or legal problems incurred abroad (see Useful Addresses). They'll notify your relatives at home, help you to receive funds, and assist with medical support.

Contact the American consulate if you have serious medical or legal trouble overseas. Although an important resource and support while you're traveling abroad, consulates will not lend you money or cash your personal check. The most they can do in this respect is to receive someone else's check or wire, and hold it for you.

American Express cardmembers can use the Global Assist Service (see Useful Addresses for phone numbers) when they have an emergency on a trip more than a hundred miles from home. The toll-free hotline will refer you to a nearby legal or medical professional, will arrange for a translator if needed, and will notify your home or office.

Know how to get emergency funds. There are several ways to get money transferred to you abroad, varying in cost and efficiency:

✓ Have a friend or relative deposit money in an account that you can access via a credit card and an ATM (automated teller machine). You'll need to know your PIN (personal identification number) code.

✓ If an ATM is not available, the Cable Remittance Order is the fastest way to send money overseas. Your home bank will transfer funds to a foreign bank, which will then notify you.

✓ The Mail Remittance order is similar, but the money is sent by air mail, not by telegram. It's much cheaper but also much slower.

✓ Western Union has an International Funds Transfer Service, through which your friend or relative can call a toll-free number, charge up to $1,000 on their Visa or MasterCard number, and have it sent to you anywhere in the country or the world. You'll be able to pick up the money at a foreign bank or post office, in local currency, one or two business days later. The person who sends the money must have the correct address.

✓ You can also go to the telegraph office wherever you are and wire your bank for money, or you can write your bank and ask it to send money to a bank in a particular city. Have your bank send a message to you at your hotel or at Poste Restante identifying the bank where the deposit has been made.

Report the loss of a credit card to the company, using its emergency phone number. If you

---

Telephoning in Emergencies

The best phoning method is to use a calling card supplied by a U.S. long-distance carrier. In countries without automatic dialing systems, your best bet is to find an international telephone and telegraph office (to be found in any major city). You give the number you wish to call to a clerk, who then dials it for you. When the connection is made, the clerk directs you to a private booth. You pay afterward.

---

report the loss immediately, before the card is used, you won't be liable for any unauthorized use. At worst, you're only liable for $50.

Report lost traveler's checks immediately, using the company's emergency phone number. Also report the loss to the police.

Report any robbery to the police and, if it occurred in a hotel, to the management. Only if you have done so will your insurance company reimburse you.

If you get arrested, contact the nearest American consulate so that you have an advocate who knows the ropes.

Don't drink and drive. Avoid even a small amount of alcohol before driving. In Scandinavia having even one drink may be considered a criminal offense if you should then cause an accident.

If you must get somewhere fast, don't accept being bumped from a flight or seriously delayed. If your plane is overbooked and you're in danger of being bumped, explain calmly and firmly to a supervisor that you cannot be bumped, that you have a confirmed seat, that you checked in at the proper time, and so on. The airline personnel are required to seek volunteers before bumping people involuntarily. If the flight is seriously delayed, explain your emergency to airline personnel and insist that, if at all possible, they find another flight for you. See Chapter 7, "Going by Plane."

What Would You Do If...

You're traveling overseas and you discover that your passport is missing.

Report a lost passport immediately to the American consulate or embassy, which can issue you a new passport (but you have to pay full price). If you have with you some passport-sized photos, a copy of your birth or naturalization certificate, and the details of your lost passport (number, date, and city of issue), this process will go much more smoothly.

If your luggage is damaged or lost, act immediately. Fill out a claim form from the airline that handled the last stage of your trip. You have seven days to claim damage and twenty-one to claim loss, but especially in the case of damage, your claim will be processed more easily if you make it immediately. See Chapter 7, "Going by Plane."

If your airplane experiences an emergency, obey your cabin crew without question. Most crashes occur during takeoff and landing, at relatively low speeds. Have your first priority be to get yourself and your children off the plane quickly. Leave everything behind. If you can leave within a minute and a half you'll probably be able to avoid the fumes that will spread through the plane. If the air is filling with fumes, stay low — crawl if necessary to avoid inhaling them. Put something over your mouth and nose if there is smoke in the cabin. And get as far as possible from the plane after the crash.

⁅16⁆

COMING HOME

A mixed brew of emotions always surfaces when you touch down on familiar ground after a trip. And, yes, there are a few final complications.

CUSTOMS

Play by the rules. Customs officials are checking for two things: dutiable items acquired abroad and illicit items not allowed into this country. Whether or not your luggage gets checked is entirely random. Therefore, if you have something you should declare, it's wise to declare it.

Do not accept packages from recent acquaintances to deliver to "friends" in the United States. Such packages have been known to contain illegal drugs.

Take the film out of your camera. A customs agent may open it.

DUTIES

Customs duties constituted, from 1789 to 1914, the main source of income for the United States government. Their purpose is to protect American products from competition with less-expensive foreign goods.

Customs officials tend to be very well versed in how much things cost. If they discover that you have undervalued something, they will confiscate it and fine you its U.S. value.

Have your receipts ready. Have handy for customs inspection receipts for any items purchased abroad. You can order a very useful booklet, *Know Before You Go,* for free from the U.S. Customs Service (see Useful Addresses, page 217).

Know the exemption limits. Every returning resident of the United States has a "personal exemption" of $400, meaning that $400 worth of goods acquired abroad may be brought into this country duty-free, subject to certain limitations on cigars, cigarettes, and liquors. Purchases must have been acquired for your personal or household use, they must be with you and declared, and your trip must have had a duration of at least forty-eight hours. No more than one hundred cigars and two hundred cigarettes (one carton) may be included in your exemption. A duty will be imposed on anything more than this. One liter (33.8 fluid ounces) of alcoholic beverages may also be brought in with you duty-free if you're twenty-one or older and it's for your own use or a gift.

Special limits apply to U.S. territories. When you return from the U.S. Virgin Islands, American Samoa, or Guam, you may bring in goods, duty-free, amounting to $800. If you're twenty-one or older you may bring in from these islands, free of duty, five liters of alcoholic beverages (169 fluid ounces). You have to have purchased four out of five of those liters on the islands, and one out of the five must have been produced there.

Duty-Free Articles

The following items are admitted free of duty:

- Antiques produced more than a hundred years ago (obtain proof of antiquity from seller)
- Binoculars, opera and field glasses
- Books
- Diamonds, cut but not set
- Drawings and paintings done entirely by hand
- Other original works of art
- Exposed film (though unexposed film may be dutiable)
- Natural pearls, loose or temporarily strung without clasp
- Postage stamps

Exceeding the exemption limits can be costly. If you exceed the above exemptions, you must pay 10 percent on the next $1,000 worth of goods (5 percent when returning from the U.S. Virgin Islands, American Samoa, or Guam).

Be careful when purchasing "works of art" overseas. Customs officials may regard them as dutiable if they were produced by a skilled craftsman instead of a professional artist. You may pay thousands of dollars for pieces of Murano glass from Italy, for example, thinking that they were created by artists and thus are duty-free, but a customs official will say they were produced by craftsmen, and thus are dutiable.

Strict criteria define "art." The key criteria are whether the work is original in concept, one of a kind, and produced by a professional artist. Anything mass-produced that you buy in a vendor's stall will not be considered a work of art. With sculpture, the original and the first ten castings are considered works of art; subsequent copies are dutiable. If you can prove that the maker of a piece is an artist, you may be able to convince customs that the item should be duty-free.

Cars purchased abroad must meet U.S. safety and emissions standards. Write the U.S. Customs Office for a leaflet called "Importing a Car."

ⅢⅢ PROHIBITED AND RESTRICTED ITEMS ⅢⅢ

Warning! Do not carry illegal drugs into or out of the United States, even though your bags have never before been searched. Customs checks are often done randomly.

Laws prohibit the following items from entering the United States:

✓ Most fruits and vegetables
✓ Most meats and poultry
✓ Absinthe

✓ Liquor-filled candy
✓ Lottery tickets
✓ Live monkeys

✓ Narcotics and dangerous drugs
✓ Publications and articles deemed by the official to be obscene, seditious, or treasonable

✓ Hazardous articles, including fireworks
✓ Toxic and poisonous items
✓ Switchblades

Special regulations govern import of some other items, including biological materials, pre-Columbian artifacts, firearms, and ammunition. Write to the U.S. Department of Agriculture (see Useful Addresses) for a free booklet called *Travelers' Tips on Bringing Food, Plant and Animal Products into the United States.*

MAILING THINGS HOME

You can ship personal belongings home if, despite your best intentions, you still brought too heavy a load with you. If you're overseas but the items were purchased in the United States, you won't have to pay duty as long as you write on the package, "American goods returned."

Inexpensive gifts can be mailed duty-free. You can send a gift valued at $50 or less to a friend duty-free, as long as the friend doesn't receive more than $50 in gift shipments in one day. Write on the outside "Unsolicited gift," what the present is, and its value. You can also send gifts to several people in one package if the gifts are individually wrapped and clearly marked.

Don't mail personal purchases. Items you purchased abroad will be dutiable if you send them to yourself.

Consider unusual alternatives. For example, in Asia, where paper and tape are in short supply, you will easily find tailors who will stitch your articles into neat cotton bundles and seal them with wax. Make sure that you clearly address the packages with indelible ink, that you firmly affix the customs forms and stamps, and that you mark the package "BY SEA" (cheap but takes forever) or "BY AIR."

ᴵᴵᴵᴵ **CULTURE SHOCK** ᴵᴵᴵᴵ

Suddenly your momentum is gone, your trip is over, and you have to resume your normal life. But your experiences have changed you. A common complaint of travelers is that no one seems interested in hearing about their extraordinary trip. (I've been fortunate to have an avid traveler for a father. Whenever I return from a trip, he'll sit down at the kitchen table and want to hear the entire story, saying "So you left here. . . . ")

Throw a party. The best way to depressurize after a trip is to give a party that includes a slide show or scrapbooks and a chance for you to discuss your trip. If you bought a cookbook, prepare an exotic dish or two. If you bought a native costume — a sari, a kimono, or a Hawaiian shirt, for example — this might be one of your few opportunities to wear it.

Start corresponding. Another way to ease culture shock is to write letters to the friends you made on your trip. If you can, send them a photo of yourself with them, or just of yourself. I've maintained such correspondences for twenty years and more. When you visit the country again, you'll have a place to go and a warm friendship to resume. You may also have a chance to host your friends in this country. Travel has given me an entirely new understanding of the concept of hospitality.

Provide feedback. You might also write letters to any organizations that helped make your trip a success — or those that did not.

ᴵᴵᴵᴵ **HEALTH** ᴵᴵᴵᴵ

Most illnesses acquired abroad will manifest symptoms during your trip or within two months of your return. If within a year you contract an illness, however, mention your trip to your doctor.

Know what to watch for. These symptoms are particularly significant: rash, prolonged fever, persistent or bloody diarrhea, inexplicable weight loss, lethargy, and unexplained pain in the abdomen, chest, or head.

17

THE SOLO TRAVELER

Both men and women often find themselves traveling alone, but women often face unique challenges. For that reason most of what follows in this chapter directly addresses the solo *woman* traveler. This shouldn't be taken to mean, however, that men won't find any useful tips below. At the very least, understanding the special difficulties women travelers face may make men readers not only better solo travelers themselves, but better companions when they travel with women.

Woman or man, solo travel is a voyage into yourself. You'll either thrive on the discoveries you make or you'll want to back out, quickly. People who intentionally travel alone have an instinctive sense that they'll enjoy it. It affords you much more interaction with the locals. You learn the language much more quickly (with a pair of traveler's, one of them often picks up the language faster and does the brunt of the talking). You'll be much closer to the reality of the country — and to the amazing goodness of other human beings.

But you may also have times when you wish you had a traveling companion with whom to share a special moment or a crisis. You can meet a companion on the road or through a service that matches travel partners (ask your travel agent about this). Many people alternate traveling alone and traveling with a partner. Before deciding to travel with someone, consult "Finding a Traveling Partner" in Chapter 1.

Begin a journal. One way to enrich a solo trip is to keep a journal. It gives you a chance to share the memorable moments and the lonely times. Many travelers later lament that they've forgotten too much about their trips. With a journal you can pin down the essence of a place — its colors, smells, sounds, scenes you witness, the food you eat, the people you meet. If you're learning a language, you can jot down particularly useful words and phrases. You can record names of hotels so you'll know which to return to and which to avoid. You can collect addresses and keep track of expenses. You won't believe how precious a document this will seem in five or ten years. Who knows — it may even be publishable.

Common sense is the key to success for the solo traveler, says a woman I know who makes frequent business trips. The less you appear to be an "out-of-towner" in big cities, she says, the better off you'll be. She always studies a map of a city she's going to. Before giving a cab driver an address, she has a general sense of how to get there. She gives the cabbie the street address, cross streets, and district, to let him know she knows where she's going. She sometimes keeps the map open on her lap to make sure he doesn't take a roundabout route. This affords a sense of security, she says, as well as sometimes reducing cab fares.

WOMEN ALONE

As a woman alone you'll experience unique challenges *and* rewards on your trip. You have more opportunities for great travel experiences than do group travelers, couples, or single men. You'll meet both women and men, in this country and abroad, much more easily than a man can. It's still unusual to see a woman traveling alone, after all, and thanks to the trust people generally feel toward women, you'll have a way into the culture that men often don't.

But it's a fine line for women travelers. A solo female can have a fabulous, incomparable trip, or she can have a disastrous one. You can meet people easily while traveling, but you may often have to extricate yourself from people you don't like or want to be with. Some women are naturally friendly and spend a lot of time putting up with and resenting unwanted companionship; others get into the habit of coldly rebuffing all approaches and then find they feel lonely and cross.

It is certainly no more dangerous to travel than it is to stay home. In foreign countries, in particular, women seem to receive more respect than they do here. The differences are that you're somewhat more exposed (in hotel rooms and campgrounds, for example) and that you do not have a native's understanding of the culture.

Do your homework beforehand. Women traveling alone must do everything, even choose their attire, with a little more care than others need. Know exactly where you're going and how to get there, so that no one can take advantage of your ignorance. Learn as much as you can about the culture, especially the status of women and the social customs. For you, a smattering of the language is especially important.

Don't let your lack of knowledge become paranoia. If you're going to be paranoid, you may as well stay home.

Don't be intimidated by odd reactions. In some countries you'll be so unusual that you'll be treated like a "third sex." In Venezuela, for example, one of the many countries where the women serve the men and then disappear into the kitchen to eat their own meals, you would undoubtedly be served with the men (and watched through the door).

Follow your instincts about men. If a man starts talking to you in the Roman Forum and you feel irritated or uncomfortable with him, don't let him attach himself to you for even a minute. Don't feel apologetic — you've invested a lot in this trip, and you should run things. Look him straight in the eye, without smiling or apologizing, and announce loudly, clearly, and firmly (in English if you don't know the language — the message will get across) that you do not wish to talk with him any more and you would like him to leave you alone. Don't worry about being rude.

Don't necessarily rebuff *all* men. If you find a man attractive or trustworthy, you're in a well-populated place, and it's daytime, you may wish to accept his offer to have a coffee. Lovely romances do happen on trips. Always pay your own way so that you don't feel obligated. Early on, find out his name and where he works. If he has a motorcycle or a car, notice the license number. And if you start feeling uncomfortable with him, disengage yourself firmly and immediately.

Do not drink heavily or take drugs with a man you've just met in a foreign country — especially if you don't know the language. This is a sure way to lose control of the situation.

Never let a strange man touch you, even in a brotherly way — except, obviously, for a handshake or a "helping hand." He may be testing your reaction. This is your cue to make an exit.

Wear a ring on your ring finger. This old trick can still get you out of a tight spot. It you wear a decorative ring, slip it around so it looks like a wedding band. Should you find yourself the object of someone's desires, just excuse yourself firmly by declaring your marital fidelity and flashing the wedding band to prove it.

Engage other women. In Third World countries, you may find that women are warm and interested in you, your trip, and your life back in America — particularly your marital status and how many children you have. Conversations with local women in some countries may revolve around these subjects, or possibly cooking or crafts. At other times you'll meet highly educated, extremely articulate, self-possessed women who will challenge you with questions about your own country.

Club Med can be a good destination for single women. It isn't cheap, but you get a great deal for the money — meals, sports instruction, entertainment, and a great location. At meals you sit at a table for eight, so you never have to eat by yourself. The ambience of the different "vacation villages" varies, however. Find out ahead of time if your degree of sophistication matches the resort's. Talk to your travel agent and also to people who have been there. (Single-parent families may also find Club Med very attractive. Children are encouraged at most of the resorts. Under the age of eight stay for free; from age eight to eleven, for half-price.)

╟╢ IN THE HOTEL ╟╢

This may be obvious, but it bears repeating. Convey a friendly but strong impression to the hotel staff. Do not flirt or be excessively familiar with male staff. This may be perceived as an invitation — to the very people who know your room number and have a master key.

170

I've experienced every nuisance from banging on my hotel room door to a stealthy trying of the knob. If this happens to you, take immediate action. If you have a telephone in your room, call the front desk and report it. If you don't have a phone, go to the door and roar, "Go away or I'll call the police!" An aggressive response on your part is generally not part of your visitor's expectations.

Guard your privacy. Consider using only your last name and first initial when registering, and discourage desk clerks from "announcing" your room number out loud when you're checking in. It's quite easy for a "lonely man" standing behind you in line to decide to call you or drop by your room.

Examine your room before you tip the bellboy. Make sure lights work, doors and windows lock, and the television operates.

Don't accept less than you deserve. Sometimes single rooms are not as attractive as doubles, and women in particular may feel they've been given a less desirable room. If the price is right, you may not mind, but if you feel it's unsatisfactory — isolated, for example, or with a panoramic view of the blank side of a building — go back to the desk clerk and ask for a different room. Make your request upon first seeing your room, not after moving in.

Don't neglect safety. A woman alone might also reject a room that's located right next to a back stairway or on the ground floor. Either of these situations makes the room too easily accessible, and is potentially dangerous. You may wish to request a room closer to the elevator (although this can be noisy in an old hotel). After finding an acceptable room, always have your key in your hand before leaving the hotel lobby to go to your room. Then you won't be fumbling in your handbag for it in an unlighted hallway.

Notice who gets on an elevator with you. Don't get on the elevator alone with a person whose looks you don't like.

If you sense you're being followed in a hotel corridor, one trick some women recommend is to bang on their own door (or even a stranger's door if necessary) and shout a man's name. Be cautious and alert, but not paranoid.

Don't swim late at night by yourself in the hotel pool. You'll be especially vulnerable there.

ⅼⅼⅼ **DINING** ⅼⅼⅼ

Many woman would love to travel solo except for the lonely prospect of sitting by themselves in restaurants day after day. Remember that being alone can be a very positive experience, even at a restaurant table. It can be an opportunity to observe people, to strike up a conversation with those at a neighboring table, to get a knowledgeable waiter's food and wine recommendation, or simply to concentrate totally on a delicious meal. A lone man doesn't appear lonely and miserable; a lone woman shouldn't feel she gives that impression either.

Don't be shy in restaurants. If you feel you've been given an inferior table (near the kitchen, for example), if the place isn't obviously crowded, and if this is important to you, politely but firmly ask for a better table. Ask to speak to the manager, if necessary.

Be prepared to go elsewhere. You're just as important as, and deserve to be treated like, any other patron. The best solution I've found to this situation is to do this: when you make your reservation or, if none is required, when you enter the restaurant, inform the maitre d' that you are a single woman and would like a good, private table. Ask if there will be any problem.

Eat a meal in your room as an alternative to eating alone in a restaurant. Take along an immersible water heater and packets of tea or instant coffee, then add fresh fruit or rolls. Room service in a nice hotel can be convenient and elegant — but expensive. Try it once.

Adapt your expectations. Don't expect things to be the way they are at home. Service may move at a slower pace than you're used to, especially in tropical countries — Central America, the Caribbean, Africa, India — and you may not have adjusted. It helps to be patient. I've known a woman who stormed out of three Indian restaurants in one hour and never realized the problem lay with her. She was simply too prickly and impatient.

Other solutions to the problem of eating alone:

✓ Bring a novel, your guidebook, or some background reading to peruse, or some postcards to write, while you await your order.

✓ Sit at a table along the wall to feel less self-conscious.

✓ Sit with another single person — and don't be surprised or offended if another single joins you, especially in Europe.

✓ If you belong to an organization, see if it has chapters (meetings, clubs, etc.) in a city you'll be visiting. Some clubs have chapters all over the world that meet regularly. Try to arrive early so that you can introduce yourself to one of the members. Before the meeting's over you'll have a host of new friends.

✓ Getting out and walking at noon or purchasing take-out food and eating in a park with office workers can be more fun than eating lunch in a restaurant.

✓ Make a tour of some good local restaurants and enjoy your meal!

PERSONAL SAFETY

Dress with dignity. Your appearance is especially important when traveling alone. Be aware of cultural norms. In many countries, women are expected to dress modestly. Although shorts and hiking boots may be acceptable vacation gear in Sweden, they would shock people in Pakistan, where women are in purdah and men normally cannot even see their eyes. In some places, the rules are not as explicit, but women dressed in jeans and T-shirts find themselves being harassed.

Show self-confidence. Unfortunately, even in a crowd you may find yourself in a difficult or annoying situation. Sometimes you have to evaluate whether to leave or make a scene. If you're the only woman in a crowd when one or more men start bothering you, be especially firm and prompt in stopping the embarrassment. In some cases, other men may come to your rescue, but don't count on it. Stay calm, look the obnoxious fellow in the eye, speak in a strong voice, and do not let the slightest self-doubt creep into your mind.

Respond firmly to unwelcome contact. An experience that befalls many female travelers in Europe is that in a very tight crowd a man will press against them in a very objectionable way. The only thing to do is to turn and push the man away from you, hard. In India there is a phenomenon called "Eve-teasing," a euphemism for when a man touches a woman improperly, usually on a bus or in a crowd. This is illegal in India; if such an incident is reported to a bus driver he's supposed to drive directly to a police station. If this does happen to you (as it may to Western women, especially those who wear Indian dress), do not ignore it. If possible, grab the offender and accost him angrily.

Don't, however, overreact. Try not to confuse the normal crush of life in a crowded country with assaults on your honor. India, for example, is a very intimate place, and you'll frequently be in close physical contact with other people.

Keep your car doors locked at all times if you're driving alone in a city. Also, roll your windows up high enough so that no one can reach in.

Think before you rest. Good places to rest while walking through a city are churches and hotel lobbies.

Keep your sense of humor. Sometimes it has to come to the rescue. I once wanted to climb the stairs to the top of a minaret to see the view of the old city surrounding a certain mosque. To my surprise and disappointment, I discovered that unescorted women could not go up in the minaret. When a bent, white-bearded, eighty-eight-year-old man gallantly offered to be my escort, I had to laugh. I realized I couldn't change centuries of Muslim tradition in five minutes, and asked a male tourist from Scotland if he would accompany me.

Women's Travel Organizations

If solo travel just isn't for you, a number of companies are ready to offer you fabulous tours with female traveling companions. For example, Earthwise Journeys, owned and operated by women, sponsors all-woman groups on an amazing variety of trips: bicycling through China, kayaking and whale-watching in Baja California, canoeing up jungle rivers in Borneo, living with a sherpa family in Nepal. The offerings range from spiritual retreats to wilderness adventures, and often include opportunities to meet local women. Refer to Useful Addresses, page 217, for more information.

|||| 18 ||||

TRAVELING
WITH CHILDREN

Traveling successfully with children depends on accepting the fact that
your trip will be very different than if you were on your own. You probably won't be pub-crawling or dancing until dawn (although you can find
excellent babysitters if you do); instead, you'll be up early watching the
barges along the Seine or enjoying the marionette show at the Tivoli
Gardens.

|||| PLANNING ||||

Let the kids help. Before the trip, it's essential to involve your children in the plans and anticipation. Let them know where you're going,
show them some colorful brochures, and describe some of the things
you'll be doing. "We'll be flying on an airplane," you might say, "until we
get to St. Louis. Then in St. Louis we'll go to a zoo, and we'll go up in a
big silver arch, and we'll see the Mississippi River." Imagine what your
children would most like to do — go to an amusement park? To a zoo
where they can pat animals? Or out in a canoe? Of course, if you
promise them you'll be doing something they find exciting, it goes without saying that you should remember to do it!

Assess your family's needs. In planning your trip, think about your
family's habits — your favorite activities, both separately and as a group,
and how you solve problems and make decisions. How well do your children get along together? Do they need constant adult supervision? Can
they get absorbed in activities for a long time or do they need to move on
to something new? How do they behave in restaurants? What do they

most like — active play? Making things? Being read to? Once you've answered these questions, you can plan your trip to accommodate the personalities involved.

Books can help. One of my favorite books, now out of print but still available in second-hand bookstores, is *Fielding's Europe with Children,* by Leila Hadley. This book would be a delight for even a nonparent to own, for it lists in detail the most "sheer fun" attractions to be found in twenty European countries from Finland to Portugal, Ireland to Greece. It includes information on flying with kids, health, water and food, diapering in a foreign land, babysitters, camps, castles, camping, and pen pals. I also recommend a marvelous service called Travel With Your Children (see Useful Addresses, page 217), which will send you, for a fee, a newsletter *(Family Travel Times)* and specific information sheets.

Plan for a homecoming party. A typically good Hadley idea is the homecoming party, to which family, close friends, and even the children's teacher and librarian are invited. Activities could include eating the food of the area, which the author suggests you send home by mail (Swiss chocolates, Scottish shortbread); listening to appropriate music; displaying and giving away the odds and ends you picked up (a beautiful shell from a Greek beach, a postcard of Paris); and, most important, viewing your slides or scrapbooks of the trip. (For more on a slide show party, see Chapter 16, "Coming Home.")

Don't Automatically Reject Exotic Destinations

Children can be great company on trips to places more exotic than this country and Europe. I know children who have traveled with their parents through India, trekked in Nepal, and viewed game in Kenya. Children speak a universal language and often bring out the very best in people. You'll see smiles shining out from otherwise impassive faces; women in particular will often relate to the kids where they'd be too shy to talk to you alone. In almost every setting in the Third World you'll find kids around or involved, so you won't feel that yours are especially loud or annoying. And reliable babysitting help is available at a very reasonable rate — check with the U.S. consulate.

Age should be a deciding factor. Remember that memories are a rich aspect of travel. Thus you might consider whether it makes sense to take a small child on an exploration of Europe when it's unlikely that he or she will remember much later. If you wait a year or two to take a big trip, those experiences will become an important part of your child's education.

Junior high school age is ideal. This can be the very best time for kids to travel with their parents. They're old enough to understand and remember what they see, yet they're not so grown up that they constantly want to escape from the family. At this age travel to an exotic place can be a profound, incomparable education. I still remember the amazement with which I experienced the bazaar in Old Jerusalem at the age of twelve.

All Places Are for Kids

As one mother puts it, if you make the destination accessible and understandable, you can take kids everywhere. For instance, in an art museum your attention may be entirely on your kids, and that can be fine if they're enjoying themselves. Show them why you like a particular painting. Give them a way into it. There might be a certain theme they could look for (ships, horses). Make a game of, for example, spotting all the dogs or cats. Talk to them in advance about what they'll see. Tell them about the artist's life. If there's one thing in a museum you particularly want to see, go there first. Otherwise, your kids' enthusiasm may wane before you get there.

Divide and conquer. When you're making your plans, you can alternate a "child's day" with an "adult's day," or an afternoon with a morning — integrating zoos with art museums, amusement parks with wineries. Or two parents can divide up the afternoon. For example, one adult can take the kids to a beach while the other goes shopping.

Don't overbudget time. The most important guideline is to slow your pace to that of your kids, not to rush them around. Plan time for resting, for eating ice cream. Expect things to take a little longer than usual. Not only will the kids be happier if you don't rush them, but you'll experience some very special moments, seeing the world through their eyes.

Children will be children. Don't let yourself be easily embarrassed by your kids in a strange place — try to understand their feelings, and be on their side.

Encourage your child to keep a diary, with thoughts and feelings about the trip as well as sketches of what he sees.

Make lunch a focus. As with all budget travelers, lunch can be your big meal. Restaurants seem more tolerant of energetic kids at lunchtime than at dinner. The same dish can be much cheaper. And your kids may be in a better mood.

Picnics are always fun, indoors and out. Whether at a rest area, a beach, a park bench, or a nice meadow by a stream, you can relax, rough-house, or just kick off your shoes and socks. You can also picnic at night in your motel room, after having your main meal at lunch. (For more on picnics, see Chapter 9, "Getting Around," and Chapter 11, "Dining.")

Try B&Bs. Bed and breakfast places that permit children are ideal for families. The atmosphere is usually much more relaxed than in a hotel or motel. Children will particularly enjoy staying on a working farm. When you call or write for reservations, mention the number of kids and their ages.

Study the language together. In a foreign country, you and the children can learn the language as a family. While you're still at home, buy a foreign language instructional tape and listen to it with the kids. For your trip, purchase a phrase book. You can quiz each other while waiting for a meal or a train. Good words to start everybody with: please, thank you, excuse me, and the numbers.

WHAT TO TAKE

Each child should have a small knapsack for personal possessions — a new book or two, pencils and paper, stickers, Play-Doh, a diary, or other toys. In the outside pocket, slip a little flashlight and a little memo pad and pen. This knapsack will be the child's own property, a place to stash any special treasures accumulated on the trip. He should help choose the toys and pack them. If he's big enough (age two and up), he should carry it himself.

Buy a few inexpensive playthings. One mother I know takes her daughter shopping a few days before the trip to purchase new pencils and other items — which she then has to save for her trip. As a result, she's always anxious to start the trip so that she can open her pack and use her new toys.

Puzzles are only fun until a piece gets lost. If you do take one, make sure it's small enough to fit on an airplane or train tray table. Count the pieces when you take them out of the box and again when you put them back in.

Take a nightlight. In addition to taking a flashlight for each child, take your own nightlight (with an adapter if you're abroad). If your baby or children awaken at night and are scared by the unfamiliar room, it may reassure them to be able to see. Also, one parent can move around and take care of problems without awakening everyone.

Take along some familiar food. For the first meals away you may wish to take food that's familiar to your toddler — breakfast cereal, for example, or a favorite kind of noodles. If a child is a fussy eater, there's no reason to believe foreign foods will help. If you're traveling to a country where sanitation may be poor, bring powdered milk to mix with boiled water for your toddler, rather than depending on local milk. (See also Chapter 4, "Health.")

Take foil-wrapped moist towelettes. Put some everywhere you might need them — in your purse, your glove compartment, your diaper bag, your carry-on bag, your kids' knapsacks, the outside pockets of your suitcases.

Also take a roll of plastic bags (removed from the box). You'll use them for soiled diapers, wet bathing suits, shoes, laundry, and a million other things.

Carry straws. Drinking straws are handy for children to use for bottled drinks, especially in less-developed countries.

Think warm. Airplanes are invariably chilly, so be sure everyone has a sweater. Trains are usually cool, as well (though occasionally you find yourself in a car that's roasting). If you're going to be on a train into the night, you might want to take blankets or sleeping bags to curl up in.

Familiar clothes are best. As with adults, children should take their favorite clothes, things they enjoy wearing. You don't want to drag around something the child refuses to put on. One mother I know buys her children a few outfits at the local department store just before a trip — coordinating, for example, wash-and-wear shorts and tops in bright colors. Clothes that don't wrinkle or show dirt easily are important. For a hot climate, the fabric should include a fair percentage of cotton.

Make packing fast. If you pack children's clothes on child-sized hangers, unpacking and packing will be much faster. (See also Packing Checklist, page 212.)

ⅠⅠⅠ EN ROUTE BY CAR ⅠⅠⅠ

Make sure to arrange for a car seat, if you have a small child, in a rental car. And be aware of laws that change from state to state and country to country. In Scotland, for example, small children cannot ride in the front seat.

Hit the road early. If you've got a long way to go and you're driving with kids, get an early start — perhaps even before they're awake — and let them sleep a few hours while you drive. Have juice and some cookies or granola bars available for when they wake up. Then stop somewhere for breakfast.

Stop frequently. Be sure to stop driving every hour and a half or two to give everyone a chance to run around, toss a football, use the bathroom, or get a drink or a snack. Anticipate tiredness and hunger. Don't get into the position of driving around looking for a restaurant when the kids are faint with hunger, or a motel when they're exhausted. If you stop driving for the day in the early afternoon, you'll have plenty of time to do something fun and find your place to stay.

Never pass up a bathroom. Throughout much of the world, the words "toilet" or WC" (water closet) will be understood. The most reliable places to find rest rooms while traveling are train and bus stations and hotels. Restaurants and coffee shops will usually have them in the back, and if your child needs to use the toilet, don't be embarrassed if you're not ordering anything to eat. In an emergency, shopkeepers may offer their facilities.

Share budget details with the kids. Let them know you have a certain amount of money to be spent every day. If they can see that you've set aside money for something like a horseback ride, it might help minimize the pleas for trinkets or coins for video games.

Take an atlas. A road atlas is not only essential but also fun. In addition to the bound maps, it has information on history, geography, landmarks, and agriculture or industry, which you can read aloud during an otherwise tedious drive. A child who can read fairly well might enjoy having his or her own road map and compass. Spend a few minutes showing your child how to use the map — the key, the index, and so on.

Also have a supply of brochures along to show the kids where they are and where they're going. Bring a cardboard file case to keep these in.

Give out travel assignments. One family I know allots different tasks to each of their children. One keeps track of the budget — how much is spent each day compared to how much was planned — and writes expenses down in a logbook. Another keeps track of the route, charting it with a colored pencil on the road map. These tasks can be fun, are great practice for the kids, and, of course, are a big contribution.

Organize "car packs." According to one imaginative mother, car packs are worth a million dollars. You can custom-make them to fit your car seats. They can hold all sorts of paraphernalia: pens, pencils, pads, pocket games, coloring books, tracing paper, dot-to-dot books, and compact (one-piece, if possible) toys. Wait until the night before a long trip to stuff the packs, one for each child. Distribute new toys for the trip among the old favorites. Then add a couple of dollars for each child as spending money. It's always fun, these parents tell us, when the children open their packs at the beginning of the trip — just like opening a Christmas stocking.

Car Pack

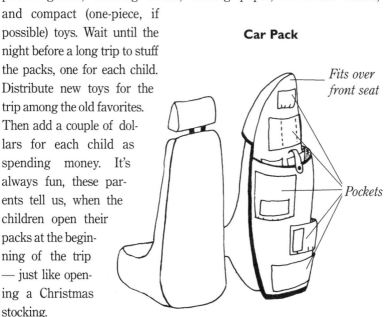

Fits over
front seat

Pockets

Provide a good writing surface. Writing on your lap in a car is difficult. "Lap desk" pillows, sold in gift shops, are ideal for the car. These are pillows that mold comfortably to the lap and are topped by a hard plastic writing surface. They can later be used at home when the child is sick in bed!

Let the kids ration their own treats. It's helpful if each child has his own little shoebox full of car treats to eat — apples, dried fruits, fresh vegetable sticks, candies to suck on. That way they won't always be clamoring to stop for snacks. Place in each box a couple of packets of small moist towelettes for wiping up sticky hands. Also be sure to take along a roll of paper towels.

Some favorite car toys: "Popomatic Bingo"; "Magic Slates"; "Pocket-Pal" games; magnetic tic-tac-toe and, for older children, chess; "Etch-a-Sketch"; quiz books with magic pens that illuminate the correct answer; funny fill-in-the-blank books; pocket quiz games; punch-out paper dolls.

Toys not to take in the car: games with little pieces, which fall and get lost, and crayons, which can melt in a hot car and smell terrible in the enclosed space. Instead, pack colored pencils (with a little portable pencil sharpener) or washable colored pens.

Invest in some high-tech equipment if you have a long drive ahead, such as a marathon drive-all-day trip across the United States. Consider electronic handheld games and a Walkman-type cassette with earphones — some families even purchase a car television and take along videotapes for the long haul. A friend's musical teenage son brought an electronic keyboard and a set of earphones on a cross-country trip. All the way across the United States he composed music and experimented with interesting sounds — which no one could hear but himself.

Tape yourself reading the children's favorite stories, if you have a cassette player with earphones. Then take with you both the books and the tapes so that the kids can listen to the stories and follow along with the books. This will save mom and dad from getting queasy trying to read aloud. Packaged book and tape combinations are more expensive, but the better ones have good orchestration and funny noises.

Let older kids "tune out." For older children, personal Walkman-type stereos are the best way to go. They can listen to their own music, not to their parents' music or their little sister's story tape. They can tune out, get to sleep more easily when they want to, and so on. Be sure they take along extra batteries.

Sing while you drive. It can be fun and funny, especially if you have a songbook for easily forgotten words. Take some blank tapes so that you can make your own tapes while driving.

Tell stories about what you're seeing, whether you're on a train or in a car. "There's a big truck from Florida and it's got oranges inside!" you might say. Or, "I see a lighthouse! Who do you think lives there?"

Trucks are eternally interesting. Take a book about trucks out of the library before your trip. Your child will enjoy learning the different types of trucks, the "anatomy" of an eighteen-wheeler, and what a truck driver's life is like. If you're at a truck stop, say hello to a driver. Your child may get a chance to see the sleeper, the gearbox, and the CB radio.

Purchase a plastic armrest with a storage compartment inside. You'll find them at auto parts stores. One or two of these could be handy for placing between siblings in the back seat, as a natural divider and a place to keep maps, books, drawing and writing materials, a travel log, and snacks.

EN ROUTE BY AIR

Make your reservations early. If you can fly at off-peak hours, your trip will be easier all around — shorter lines, more room on the aircraft — and you'll have the best chance of getting a free seat for your infant or toddler.

Children up to age two can travel free on most airlines. They are not, however, guaranteed seats, although airline personnel may make an effort to keep an empty seat next to a parent with a "lap baby." If you're tempted to tell the airline that a child is under two, when he or she is actually older, remember that if the plane is full you'll be sitting with that child on your lap throughout the entire flight. One trip across the Atlantic with a twenty-five-pound child in your lap, plus all the paraphernalia, with only one meal to share between you, may convince you to pay for the child's seat next time.

Ask for early seat selection, especially if you're traveling with an infant. Although the airline may automatically give you a bulkhead seat,

I find that regular aisle seats are more convenient. You have more luggage stowing space, and there are fold-down tables (not always present in bulkhead seating). You can get up when you need to, and you can stretch out your feet in the aisle. The advantage to bulkhead seats is that you can have your own little world there, especially good for toddlers, who can color or play with puzzles at your feet and can even stretch out and nap there.

Reading will help prepare small children. A week or so before the trip, take a book about airplanes out of the library and read it to or with your child.

To make flying with infants and toddlers a little easier, try the following tips:

✓ A lightweight collapsible "umbrella" stroller is handy for the airport all the way up through the jetway or across the tarmac to the door of the aircraft. At that point, it can be stored in the front of the plane (for no extra charge). Just don't forget it when you disembark!

✓ On a night flight, take your child in pajamas, and then change her into day clothes before you land. On overnight flights, take the child's nightwear and change her into it once you're on board.

✓ Any familiar "going-to-bed" rituals, such as snuggling a stuffed animal or hearing a bedtime story, will help induce sleep.

✓ Remind your child not to kick the seat in front of him. Explain that this is extremely annoying to the person sitting there.

✓ If you wish your baby to use a "skycot" — an airplane bassinet — be sure to reserve it in advance. All airlines have a few of these available for babies. Otherwise, you can bring your baby's carry-cot free of charge, with diapers, blankets, a change of baby clothes, and a supply of baby food.

✓ It's easiest if you carry your own baby food with you. If, however, you order twenty-four hours in advance, the airline will provide a baby meal of strained meat and vegetables, but you should still have your own supply of milk, juice, crackers, fruit, cheese, or yogurt. Put food in little jars or plastic containers that you can throw away after you've used them.

✓ The flight attendant will warm a baby bottle for you. Try to anticipate when your baby will need it, so he isn't crying for it when the rest of the passengers are being served.

✓ Make sure your carry-on luggage contains everything you'll need not only on the plane but also for the first twenty-four hours of your trip. If you're traveling with a baby, include disposable diapers (the airplane may have a small supply, but don't count on it), a bib, plenty of baby juices, disposable towels, a change of clothes for the baby, and a cloth diaper to lay her on while she's being changed.

✓ Most airplanes don't provide a good place to change a baby (although this is slowly changing). Ask the flight attendant if there's a row of empty seats where you can change him. Otherwise, you'll have to use your seat or the aisle.

✓ During takeoff, hold your infant or toddler on your lap, outside your seat belt, even if there's an empty seat next to you (unless, of course, you have a car seat with you).

✓ As the plane takes off and lands, the change in cabin pressure affects the eustachian tubes. To equalize the pressure behind the ear drums, you and older children can yawn vigorously and chew gum, or close your mouths, hold your noses, and try to blow softly. Your baby, however, may suffer earaches. The best solution is to let the baby nurse or drink from a bottle or a cup during takeoff and landing (this might even put him to sleep!)

✓ Have in your diaper bag enough juice to last through the flight. The cabin air will be very dry and babies especially can become dehydrated.

⑩ EN ROUTE BY TRAIN ⑩

Trains are the ideal way to travel with children. There's plenty to do and see, both out the window and on the train. Where planes quickly become nothing more than a confined space with no view, trains have the best scenery and lots of room to walk around.

Think ahead about seating. Look at your route on a map ahead of time, so that you know what towns and landmarks you'll be passing. This can guide you in choosing which side of the train to sit on. If you're going by train from New York City to Montreal, for example, sit so that the kids can look out at the Hudson River. When traveling with kids, the best places to sit are near other kids, near the bathroom, and near the snack bar.

Give your child the best view. If you let your child sit in the window seat and you take the aisle seat, her attention will be directed more toward the world passing outside than to the other passengers, and you can monitor her comings and goings.

Don't dress up. Trains and train stations are grimier than planes and airports. Have the kids dress in jeans rather than in "Sunday best." If you want them to look fresh and neat upon arrival, they can change into clean clothes in the rest room before you reach your destination.

Take a carry-on. Even when traveling by train, where your suitcases are normally within reach above your seat, it makes sense to have a carry-on bag. This can hold snacks, juice, diaper supplies, a change of clothes for your child, and possibly an extra toy to surprise him with when he's played with all of those he packed himself in his knapsack.

Take food along. If you have room in your luggage, take a picnic basket packed with sandwiches, fruit, crackers, and other snacks. Your child can purchase drinks. Food is expensive on a train.

Your baby can travel in a carry-cot, which will allow her to watch the world flashing by or drift off to sleep — you won't even have to awaken her upon arrival at your destination. This is much easier and more comfortable than having her sleep on your lap or on the seat itself.

ⅲ UNACCOMPANIED MINORS ⅲ

Children between the ages of eight and eleven can travel alone on Amtrak if their trip will be completed in the daytime and if they won't be changing trains. They must, however, receive approval from the general manager of the station of origin. Children twelve and up can travel overnight.

On airplanes, children between five and seven can make a direct flight alone. Children eight and up can fly unaccompanied with one change. The person meeting the child must have identification and, in some cases, a prearranged code word. Frequently airlines charge a small fee to cover the extra service. A child escort service can be arranged to assist the child through customs, passport, and security.

What Would You Do If...

You are separated from your child in a crowded place.

It is important to think about this possibility before you take a trip.

- *Talk as a family about what you want the children to do if this happens.*
- *Teach your children not to wander around looking for you, but to stop and stay in a visible spot, to be more easily found. You may even wish to practice this in your local supermarket.*
- *Teach your children to ask a police officer (or other uniformed person) for help.*
- *Before entering a crowded place, look for and choose a "findingplace": the entry gate to a zoo, a tall prominent structure in a public square, an information booth.*
- *Have your children wear something that will make it easy for you to spot them from far away. The color red has helped my family stay together in many crowd scenes. Consider purchasing red jackets, sweatshirts, or T-shirts for your children.*

▏19▕

THE OLDER OR DISABLED TRAVELER

Travel no longer belongs only to the young and able bodied. In fact, senior or disabled travelers often have especially wonderful trips, simply because they have to have an extra helping of the very qualities that make travel successful — resourcefulness, adventurousness, cheerfulness, a sense of humor, and careful planning.

▏ THE OLDER TRAVELER ▕

Senior citizens and retirees have become a major part of the traveling public, and the travel industry is courting them with a wide array of discounts and special deals. As always, however, you must ask for your discount or you may not receive it. To facilitate things, carry identification with proof of your age and membership in senior organizations.

Foreign travel is an excellent bet for the older person. In most other countries of the world, you will find, older people are far more honored than they are in the United States.

Join the AARP. If you're fifty, you can join the American Association of Retired Persons. This organization has a travel service (see Useful Addresses, page 217) that designs tours, cruises, and holiday packages especially for senior travelers. In addition, the membership card will allow you to receive discounts for some airlines, many hotels, rental cars, and more. Membership in the AARP is extremely cheap, so there's no reason not to join!

Check out other senior groups. Another wonderful organization that caters only to older travelers is Elderhostel (see Useful Addresses). Through it you can study at universities and colleges all over the world.

Send for specialized information. The U.S. Government Printing Office will send you, for a small fee, its booklet *Travel Tips for Mature Citizens*. A free booklet entitled *101 Tips for the Mature Traveler* is available from Grand Circle Travel. Refer to Useful Addresses.

Fly off-peak. If you're a retiree you may have a flexible schedule that permits you to travel at off-peak hours. This way you can avoid the stress of long lines and you may also save money. Try to fly midweek, midday, or Saturday. Avoid traveling on Mondays and Fridays, which are heavy travel days.

Get your seat assigned early. Thirty days before your departure date, call the airline for an advance seat assignment. The most comfortable and accessible seats are on the aisle and toward the front of the aircraft. The bulkhead seats have extra legroom, but remember that you may be sitting next to parents with babies.

Travel light. You want to be sure that you can carry all your belongings yourself when you need to. For walking through the airport, portable wheels on your suitcase are handy, but make sure that they won't be cumbersome for the many times you'll have to carry your bag (getting into buses and cabs, climbing stairs, getting over curbs).

Get to the airport early. Plan to arrive at the airport in plenty of time — at least an hour ahead of departure time for domestic flights, and two hours ahead for overseas flights. Watch the television monitors for information on departure times and gate assignments. Most airlines offer early boarding to older passengers needing assistance.

Wear comfortable clothing for the flight. Bring along some slipper socks to wear, and an eyeshade or ear plugs if the muted din of an airplane will disturb you.

Pamper yourself while you're on your trip, perhaps with a down pillow — you can buy one that will squash down to nothing in your suitcase. You'll find that being able to indulge in a familiar custom in a strange surrounding will provide a sense of security, even luxury. One of my grandmothers traveled the world with a packet of good tea and a bone china teacup wrapped up in her lingerie.

Be prepared for snafus. One experienced traveler we know recommends that you run through in your mind all the potential snafus of your trip. Then visualize how you might cope with them. In many cases, proper planning can alleviate your anxieties. For example, if you're concerned about missing a plane connection, schedule extra time between flights — two hours may be better than one. If you're concerned about getting around with your baggage, either pack very light or bring along a set of collapsible wheels that can be folded up when not needed. If you're concerned about health emergencies, join an "assistance" plan (see Chapter 4, "Health"). Think through all such potential problems and anticipate their solutions.

Look for senior discounts. Many discounts exist if you ask for them and have proof of your age. For example, those over sixty-two and disabled travelers receive 25 percent off all regular Amtrak fares.

Know Your Health Coverage

Medicare won't pay health expenses incurred abroad. You may, however, have adequate health and travel insurance through Blue Cross/Blue Shield policies, your homeowner's policy, or some of the special travel insurance policies offered by some credit card companies. If you think you do, check the benefit details carefully, because some policies have geographic exclusions.

THE DISABLED TRAVELER

The sheer number of wheelchair travelers has prompted the travel industry to compete for the disabled market. There's a wealth of guidebooks and services available, airports and hotels become more accessible every day, and dozens of travel agencies now specialize in vacations for the disabled traveler. So much is possible — we have friends who have traveled in wheelchairs through South America, Africa, and India, as well as Europe and North America.

Listed under Useful Addresses (see page 217) you'll find the names of some excellent services. If, however, you'd like to make your own arrangements, or if you're headed somewhere exotic that isn't covered in a guidebook, here are a few tips to keep in mind while planning:

✓ Have your wheelchair checked by a wheelchair mechanic before you go. Bring along a tool kit and spare axle.

✓ Travel at less busy times — midweek, midday, Saturday.

✓ Tell the reservations clerk of your disability.

✓ Take a nonstop or direct flight so that you need not change planes.

✓ Arrive at the airport early. You will "preboard" the plane.

✓ Put a baggage tag on your wheelchair, which will probably be transported in the baggage compartment. Make sure it will be brought to the door of the plane when you reach your destination, and not to the baggage claim.

✓ Crutches and canes may be stowed under your seat if they don't stick out into the aisle.

✓ Guide and hearing dogs can travel on board a plane with their owners, free of charge. They're supposed to sit or lie at your feet. If you're going to a foreign country, however, there may be a quarantine that applies to your dog.

Questions to Ask When Making an Airline Reservation

- Does the airline have any special requirements? For example, will it require that you be accompanied? Sometimes the airline will waive such a requirement if you seem competent and confident.

- What type of aircraft is it — wide-bodied or narrow-bodied?

- Where will your wheelchair be stowed?

- Does the particular flight have jetways for boarding and disembarking? If not, how will you get on and off the plane? Some airlines have a narrow boarding chair; others use a lift.

- Are special seats assigned to wheelchair passengers?

- Are the restrooms accessible? If you cannot walk, you may require assistance. (Future airplane rest rooms will probably be designed to accommodate wheelchairs.)

Airline personnel are there to serve you. Be sure they do just that. The pilot should radio ahead if you'll need assistance during or after deplaning, and an escort will help you pass through customs and immigration.

Patronize responsible establishments. Many hotel chains now have a policy of accessibility. It makes sense to patronize those companies that have made this effort. The chains include Holiday Inn, Hyatt, Sheraton, Hilton, Marriott, Howard Johnson, and Quality Inns.

Take advantage of fare breaks. In this country, Greyhound offers special plans that allow one disabled person and one companion to travel for a single fare. Amtrak gives disabled individuals a 25 percent discount.

Research accessibility. Write for a free copy of *Access Travel: A Guide to Accessibility of Airport Terminals,* from the Consumer Information Center (see Useful Addresses).

Questions to Ask When
Making a Hotel Reservation

■ Is there special disabled parking?

■ Are there ramps from the parking area to the sidewalk and then into the building?

■ How far will your room be from the elevator?

■ How wide are the doorways into the rooms and bathrooms? Twenty-six inches is minimum.

■ Are there grab bars at toilet and tub?

■ If you're traveling alone, how high are the light switches?

20

TRAVELING
ON BUSINESS

Business travelers have different priorities, and more need of genuine savvy, than recreational travelers do. You need to get places fast, economically, efficiently; your travel arrangements and connections must be smooth enough so as not to distract you from the primary focus of your trip.

The business traveler is the bread and butter of the travel industry — you put in the long miles, the numerous nights in hotels, and the business meals at all hours of the day or night.

Because the travel industry too often assumes that the business traveler operates on a fat travel budget, it's harder to find bargain rates and attractive discounts, particularly on hotels. Uncovering the best rate for business travel arrangements requires flexibility and some intelligent probing.

Cultivate a travel agency. Develop a good relationship with a travel agency that has a business travel expert who can find you the cheapest and fastest flight, a decent and convenient room that won't bankrupt you, and a rental car without hassles.

Or train your own. If you feel it's impossible to get the service or savings you need through a travel agent, you may wish to train someone in your firm to handle travel arrangements. This person will need toll-free reservation numbers, a pad of paper, some time to spend, and the combination of patience and persistence that always wins the best deal.

Know what weather to expect. Be sure to plan your route with an eye on weather conditions. If you want to go to Las Vegas and you have a choice of going via Chicago or via Atlanta, take into account possible weather-related delays. Call 900-WEATHER for information on weather in domestic and foreign cities.

Seek discounts. Always ask for the corporate discount, and double-check when you pick up your room key or rental car. It's always best to have asked at the beginning of the transaction rather than at the end.

Pack light, pack smart. A relative who spends a good deal of time on the road for business recommends that you save the plastic bags your dry cleaner provides. When laying out the clothes for your trip, separate out everything that easily wrinkles — fine cottons, silks, woolens, and delicate fabrics. Put one or two of these items on a hanger, cover them with a dry cleaner's bag, and pack them that way in your luggage. The plastic prevents wrinkles, and all you have to do when you arrive is reach into your suitcase and hang up your clothes!

Treat your feet well. Take along a second pair of comfortable shoes if you'll be on your feet for more than one day — for example, at a trade show.

⁞⁞⁞ AIRLINES ⁞⁞⁞

Get price quotes from at least three different airlines. Don't forget to check with Canadian airlines, which, in my experience, offer very competitive fares.

Join a frequent flyer club or two if you travel a good deal on business. The airline will give you an account number and keep a log of the miles you fly with them. When you reach a certain number of miles the airline will reward you with a bonus — for example, after twenty thousand miles they may give you a free upgrade from coach to first class; after thirty thousand, a free ticket. If you're married, both you

Further Information
See also Questions to Ask When Making Airplane Reservations, page 204.

and your spouse should join frequent flyer clubs, for added discounts. Hotels and rental car agencies have also gotten into the act: after you've flown a certain number of miles you may be able to rent a car with unlimited mileage, for example, or a free hotel room.

Arrive early. Always plan to arrive the night before your meeting, or earlier if you'll be coping with jet lag. Avoid scheduling a meeting in Hong Kong followed two days later by a meeting in Paris, or one in San Francisco followed closely by one in New York. You'll be able to make the meetings, but your performance will be seriously hampered by jet lag. See Chapter 7 for information on jet lag.

Try remaining on hometown time throughout the trip if you must make several meetings in different parts of the world. This is the technique made famous by President Lyndon Johnson on political trips around the world.

Get your seat assigned early. When you make your flight reservation, obtain your seat assignment as early as possible. Most business travelers prefer a seat on the aisle far up front in the aircraft, so that they can get

Tips to Maximize Frequent Flyer Benefits

- When choosing a frequent flyer program, consider the airlines that fly to the areas where you're most likely to go.

- Find out what the minimum prize level is — for some it's ten thousand miles, and for others it's twenty thousand.

- Tie-ins with hotels and car rental agencies yield lucrative points. Use these associated companies.

- Keep your own record of the number of miles you've flown. Some travelers find errors in the log the airline supplies.

- Have your spouse and any traveling children (college or boarding-school students) join the program as well.

off the plane quickly after landing. When you fly on a small commuter plane, especially, sit next to the door. Most or all of your fellow passengers will be business travelers and will race for the first available cabs.

Consider requesting a bulkhead seat. On full-sized aircraft, bulkhead seats have the most room for spreading out your work. Be forewarned, however, that these seats are often assigned to parents traveling with children. If you have a low tolerance for crying babies, you'd better sit farther back or take along some ear plugs!

Purchase a pocket airport guide. One available from AM Data Service (see Useful Addresses, page 217) includes diagrams for more than seventy-five major U.S. airports, showing locations of ticket counters, gates, baggage claims, and car rentals.

Avoid checking bags. Because you need to travel fast and light, avoid luggage check-in wherever possible. Use a fold-over garment bag, which can carry socks and shoes as well as suits, and a briefcase big enough to hold a toilet kit. Your garment bag can be carried on board and hung in a cabinet, rather than checked with other luggage.

Never check essential materials. Always carry your laptop computer, briefcase, presentation, and slides on the plane with you. Include in your briefcase a minidesk set containing scissors, clips, transparent tape, stapler, calculator, dictation recorder, and any other items you frequently use.

Guard your computer en route. Be vigilant. Computers are among the most commonly stolen items at airports. (And remember you can't use your laptop during takeoff and landing.)

Airport parking is a nuisance. If you'll be away more than a few days, take a shuttle or limousine service to the airport, rather than using the airport parking lot. If a shuttle or limousine isn't available, find a park-and-ride service. Most hotels in the vicinity of airports now offer this service, which may not only be cheaper but also faster than using the airport's long-term lot. The service will deliver you to your departure gate and pick you up at the baggage claim area. Some of these companies even have your car started, cleaned off, and warmed up in winter months — a real bonus.

Know how to deal with delays. Before leaving for the terminal, telephone the airline to see if your flight is on time. At the first sign that your flight may be held up or delayed, don't waste time standing in line at the ticket counter if this will create a problem for you. Find the nearest phone. First telephone your own airline (use its toll-free number or a courtesy phone) and ask what the story is and when your flight will be leaving. Then, if necessary, make inquiries with other airlines to see if you can get on another flight that will be leaving directly.

ⅢⅠ CAR RENTAL ⅢⅠ

Ask or you won't receive. Ask the agent for the best deal or you won't get it. Also ask where the lot is in relation to your terminal. Find out if a regular shuttle service runs between the lot and the terminal.

Don't duplicate insurance. Check your own personal and corporate insurance coverage before paying for costly insurance on a rental car. You may already be adequately covered.

Carefully examine your rental. Before accepting a rental car, inspect the vehicle completely for possible undetected damage that could be charged to you upon return. Should you spot any problem, be sure the agent notes it on the rental agreement.

Check your bags before returning the car. When you return a rental car to an airport terminal, check your luggage (except carry-on items) at curbside

Further Information
See also Questions to Ask Before Renting a Car, page 205.

before taking the car back to the parking lot. Double-check that your bags are properly labeled and tagged, return the car to the correct lot, and take a shuttle back to the terminal.

ᴵᴵᴵᴵ HOTELS ᴵᴵᴵᴵ

When looking for a hotel, consider convenience, shuttle service to and from the airport, quiet, cleanliness, price, and extended room service hours. Check out the new inexpensive chains designed for the business traveler.

Ask what kind of recreational facilities the hotel offers — swimming pool, gym, spa, or tennis court — to help pick you up after a long flight or unwind after a stressful meeting. Also ask if there are popular restaurants and theaters within walking or cab distance. Entertainment can be an important element of a successful business trip.

Use express check-out. When you check in at a hotel, ask if it offers express check-out service. This can be a big timesaver, but you won't see the bill until you get home. You simply drop off your room key at a designated place, and your bill gets mailed to your business address. Any problems with the bill must be settled through the mail or over the phone.

Further Information
See also Questions to Ask When Making a Hotel Reservation, page 206.

Always examine your hotel bill carefully, either when you check out or when you receive the bill in the mail. If you charge services to your hotel room, you can quickly verify the bill's accuracy with the following system. Add a tip or arrange the final charges so that the last digit always ends in the same number. For example, let's say you use "4" as the code number. If you have drinks at the bar, add a tip so that the total comes out to $15.54. If you get room service, add a tip so that the charges add up to $10.34; or add a few pennies to your parking charges so that the cost will be $22.04. When you scan your bill at the end of your stay, it will be immediately apparent which services you actually charged.

⊦⊦⊏⊣⊓⊔⊦⊣ ⊓ ⊓ ⊏ ⊔⊏⊔⊔⊔⊏⊓⊏⊓⊏⊓⊏

Because business travel can be very stressful, take special care of your physical needs.

Try to exercise every day, using the hotel pool or gym if there is one, or simply by taking a brisk morning walk.

Eat prudently, and get enough sleep to keep you alert and on your toes.

Join IAMAT. If business takes you abroad, join the International Association for Medical Assistance to Travelers (see Useful Addresses). It's free! This organization was founded more than thirty years ago to help travelers cope with medical problems overseas. In particular, IAMAT makes competent medical advice available to travelers around the world by doctors who speak English or French and were trained in Europe or North America.

Making the Most of It

You've been in meetings all day and you're exhausted. Your host or a business associate asks if you'd like to see a little of the city before turning in. You're wondering if you should politely accept or call it a day.

Be curious about the place you're visiting. If your host offers to show you around, don't pass it up. It can add depth and context to your business deal. It might even launch a valuable friendship.

▥ GIVE FEEDBACK ▥

An experienced business traveler has contact with more travel-related personnel and services than any other type of traveler. When you receive exceptional service — either good or bad — don't hesitate to put your thoughts down in a letter to the customer service director. You can get this person's name by calling the firm's toll-free number, asking for the number of the customer service department, and then calling that number for the director's name and correct address. Explain in your letter the circumstances of your trip. You can generally expect a prompt and courteous response.

If the service was very good, a letter of commendation is one of the nicest gestures one professional person can give another. But if you were mistreated or your accommodations were unsatisfactory, that will be acknowledged in the reply, and some kind of compensation will usually be made to restore your faith in the company and its product.

CHECKLISTS

What follows is a number of checklists to help you with your planning. Photocopy these forms, if you wish, and make a trip folder. I've found it very helpful to keep all important information together in one place. You may wish to add things to these checklists that you feel are important, and ignore items that don't concern you.

QUESTIONS TO ASK WHEN MAKING AIRPLANE RESERVATIONS

Is that the lowest fare? Are alternative seatings available and cheaper?

Will I get a better fare if I fly mid-week or Saturday?

Is there a corporate rate?

Is there a discount available for frequent flyers? Retired persons? Students? Children? Military?

May I have an upgrade based on my frequent flyer points?

Is this the only airline serving this airport?

Are there any good standby possibilities?

Would it be cheaper to fly into or out of an adjacent airport?

What are the restrictions? When do I need to make my reservation? Purchase my ticket? Is there a penalty if I cancel?

Is it a nonstop flight? Direct? What are the stops and how long will they be? If it is a connecting flight, do I have at least forty-five minutes to make my connection?

What are the flight numbers?

What type of aircraft is it?

May I have my seat assignment now? aisle _____; window _____; smoking _____; nonsmoking _____; far forward _____.

Will a meal be served? Will there be a movie shown?

Note: *Write down the name of the clerk, the date, and the time.*

ⅲⅰ QUESTIONS TO ASK BEFORE ⅲⅰ RENTING A CAR

What's the best deal? The best weekend deal? Any specials?

What is the mileage charge?

Is there a corporate rate?

Can the car be picked up at the airport? Where is the lot in relation to the terminal? Is there a shuttle service to and from the terminal?

Can the car be dropped off at the airport? Can it be dropped off in another city, and if so, is there a charge for this?

How much for insurance (total)? Will my own insurance policy cover this?

Is there a special rate for certain types of cars? For members of certain organizations? For extended travel?

What is the car make and model? Is it a luxury car? Jeep? Van? Camper?

Does the car have any special features? air conditioning ___ ; front-wheel drive ___ ; hand controls or wheelchair ramp ___ ? infant car seat ___ ; If it's a station wagon or hatchback, does it have a panel that conceals luggage packed inside ___ ?

What is the confirmation number?

Note: *If you are renting a car in another country, make sure that there are no age restrictions.*

ꡙ QUESTIONS TO ASK WHEN MAKING ꡙ A HOTEL RESERVATION

What is the daily rate? The weekly rate? Other special rate?

Is there a corporate discount? A discount for retired persons? For families?

Is the hotel a participant in any frequent flyer programs?

Is there a surcharge for a single traveler?

Are there any "perks" for frequent guests?

Where is the hotel located — in the business district (convenient to where appointments are)? In a quiet part of town? Within walking or cab distance of popular restaurants or theaters? On the beach? Near the beach? Near the ski slopes?

Does public transportation serve the hotel?

What are the parking arrangements? What is the daily parking rate?

Is there a restaurant in the hotel?

What are the room service hours?

Does the hotel have recreational facilities — pool? hot tub? sauna? fitness club? tennis court? other?

What are the fire safety precautions? What floor will the room be on?

When is check-out time? Is there an express check-out service?

What is the confirmation number?

⑂⑂ SAFETY NUMBERS LIST ⑂⑂

PASSPORT(S)

Name	Passport No.	City of Issue	Date

AIRPLANE TICKET(S)

Airline	Flight No.	Date	Departs City/Time	Arrives City/Time	Ticket No.

TRAVELER'S CHECKS

Issuing Company _____ Emergency Phone No. _____

Denomination	Amount	Numbers	to

CREDIT CARD(S)

Company	Number	Expiration Date	Emergency Phone No.

HOMETOWN TRAVEL AGENT

Telephone No. _____

HOMETOWN BANK

Telephone No. _____ Account No. _____

Address_____

_____

ⅼⅼⅼ GETTING READY — A CHECKLIST ⅼⅼⅼ

Every step of preparation for a trip can be exciting, yet all too often things get put off until the last minute, when you're in a mad rush. Here's a schedule to guide you in readying everything for a big trip in plenty of time.

Twelve to three months before departure date (depending on where and how you're going):

- ❏ Make plane, boat, and /or train reservations.
- ❏ Buy a guidebook or two that focus on the areas you'll visit.
- ❏ Start developing your itinerary.
- ❏ Inquire about hotel rates and make reservations.
- ❏ Obtain an International Certificate of Vaccination from the U.S. Public Health Department or a Passport Agency.

Four months before departure date:

- ❏ Have passport photos taken.
- ❏ Find out about car rental, train passes, other internal travel arrangements.
- ❏ Begin learning the language. Purchase a phrase book or instructional tape.

Three months before departure date:

- ❑ Apply for passport and, once you have your passport, visas.
- ❑ Schedule an appointment with your physician for four to six weeks before you leave. You'll need a complete physical exam. You should also determine if you need any shots, including a tetanus booster, and/or medication.
- ❑ Make an appointment for a dental checkup and cleaning.

Two months before departure date:

- ❑ Call or write the consulates of the countries or the state tourist departments of the states you'll be visiting for tourist information.
- ❑ Make a list of the things you'll take with you.
- ❑ Begin collecting addresses of people you know living abroad.
- ❑ Examine insurance policies. Take out additional coverage if desired. Make sure auto, fire, and other policies are up to date.
- ❑ If you need new shoes for the trip, buy them now, and start breaking them in.

One month before departure date:

- ❑ If you haven't received your passport and visas by now, you should inquire.
- ❑ Order foreign currency ($50–$100 worth) through your bank for your needs upon arrival.
- ❑ Call the airline for advance seat assignment.
- ❑ Have prescriptions filled for extra glasses, contact lenses, or any medications you might need.
- ❑ Have a complete physical examination.
- ❑ If you're going to be inoculated against typhoid, you must have your first shot now, and your second shot in four weeks. If you need a yellow fever shot, you may get it now also.
- ❑ Make plans to board your pets, have your lawn mowed or driveway plowed, and have your mail picked up.
- ❑ Telephone your travel agent to find out when you may pick up your ticket.

Two weeks before departure date:

❑ Contact a reliable neighbor or friend and let them know you'll be gone. Arrange to leave this person your itinerary, car license number, and a house key. Confirm this person's address and telephone number.

❑ Double-check all travel arrangements, to make sure you haven't forgotten anything.

❑ Take clothes to the dry cleaner, if necessary.

One week before departure date:

❑ Pick up your traveler's checks and tickets, if possible.

❑ Arrange to discontinue newspaper, milk, UPS, and other deliveries until further notice. Arrange for the post office to hold your mail if no one will pick it up for you.

❑ Inform your police department of when you're leaving and when you're returning. Let the police know a neighbor has your house key.

❑ Make a trial pack to see if everything fits.

❑ Start taking antimalarial medication.

Three days before departure date:

❑ Confirm your international flight.

❑ Pick up tickets, if you haven't received them yet.

❑ Gather items to be packed. Make sure everything is clean, has working batteries, and so on. If you're the last-minute type, pack now.

Two days before departure date:

❑ Get your gamma globulin injection against hepatitis.

One day before departure date:

❑ Pack.

❑ Confirm your domestic flight; reconfirm your international flight if you wish. Write down date, time, and name of agent you speak with.

Three hours before departure:
- ❑ Call airport to find out whether your flight is on time.

Two to three hours before departure:
- ❑ Arrive at airport and check in.

Half an hour before departure:
- ❑ Arrive at gate.
- ❑ Set watch or alarm clock to destination time.

Bon voyage!

ⅲ PACKING CHECKLIST ⅲ

This list is for a recreational trip. Don't bring everything listed here — just those items that make sense to you. Consider this amount to be packing light, but not extra light. See Chapter 5, "What to Take," for the latter.

Clothes
- ❑ 2 pairs pants — at least one sturdy and one that's suitable for dress occasions. Fabric should contain some cotton.
- ❑ 3–4 shirts. If you'll be in the tropics, at least one shirt should be long-sleeved to protect against sunburn and mosquitoes. Fabric should contain a fair percentage of cotton.
- ❑ Sweater — dark color best (wear en route)
- ❑ One skirt for dress occasions, for comfort en route and in the tropics
- ❑ One sports jacket for men — some restaurants require them
- ❑ Swimsuit
- ❑ Cover-up for beach or pool
- ❑ Raincoat and galoshes
- ❑ Hat — beret or sun hat
- ❑ 3–5 pairs underwear
- ❑ 5 pairs socks — cotton or wool
- ❑ Sleepwear

We'd love your thoughts...

Your reactions, criticisms, things you did or didn't like about this Storey Book. Please use space below (or write a letter if you'd prefer — even send photos!) telling how you've made use of the information . . . how you've put it to work . . . the more details the better! Thanks in advance for your help in building our library of good Storey Books.

Pamela B. Art

Publisher

Book Title: _____

Purchased From: _____

Comments: _____

_____

_____

_____

_____

_____

_____

_____

_____

Your Name: _____

Address: _____

☐ Please check here if you'd like our latest Storey's Books for Country Living Catalog.

☐ You have my permission to quote from my comments, and use these quotations in ads, brochures, mail, and other promotions used to market your books.

Signed _____   Date _____

email=Feedback@Storey.Com   PRINTED IN USA   10/95

From: _____

BUSINESS REPLY MAIL

FIRST CLASS MAIL   PERMIT NO. 2   POWNAL, VT

POSTAGE WILL BE PAID BY ADDRESSEE

STOREY'S BOOKS FOR COUNTRY LIVING
STOREY COMMUNICATIONS, INC.
105 SCHOOLHOUSE ROAD
POWNAL VT 05261-9988

❑ 1 pair sturdy, well-broken-in shoes. (Buy sandals in the tropics, walking shoes in Ireland and the U.K., dress shoes in France and Italy.)

Winter Travel
❑ Down jacket
❑ Boots, well waterproofed
❑ Gloves and hat
❑ Long underwear

Other Essentials — all are small enough to fit in large purse or carry-on
❑ Passport
❑ Tickets
❑ Itinerary
❑ Traveler's checks
❑ International Certificate of Vaccination
❑ Maps
❑ Knife with bottle and can opener and corkscrew (if desired)
❑ Money belt or pouch
❑ Extra glasses, contact lenses, prescriptions
❑ Combination lock
❑ Address book
❑ Day pack — invaluable to carry your things when you take a day trip or leave your bags at Left Luggage; to carry picnics or laundry; to hold camera and film when you pass through security points; as an extra carry-on
❑ Journal
❑ Small pad of paper
❑ Pocket flashlight for each person
❑ Net shopping bag
❑ Travel alarm clock
❑ Sunglasses
❑ Pens and pencils
❑ Camera, film, batteries, lens covers, lens tissues
❑ Roll of zip-closure bags
❑ Dictionary and/or phrase book

Laundry Supplies

- ❏ Laundry detergent in small packets or tubes — Woolite or Prell
- ❏ Stretchable clothesline with six small clothespins
- ❏ Small clothesbrush
- ❏ Inflatable hanger or two
- ❏ Rubber sink stopper
- ❏ Plastic bags

First-Aid Kit

- ❏ Bandages
- ❏ Moleskin for blisters
- ❏ Analgesic
- ❏ Foil-wrapped antiseptic towelettes
- ❏ Suntan lotion
- ❏ Insect repellent
- ❏ Tincture of iodine
- ❏ Antimalarial pills
- ❏ Mosquito netting
- ❏ Thermometer in hard case
- ❏ Nail clipper
- ❏ Tweezers

Toilet Articles

- ❏ Toothbrush and paste, extra dental floss
- ❏ Soap and soapdish
- ❏ Shampoo — Prell is good for many different uses (see page 53)
- ❏ Moisturizer
- ❏ Lip balm
- ❏ Small towel and washcloth
- ❏ Hairbrush and/or comb
- ❏ Razor, blades, and shaving cream

Optional

- ❏ Ear plugs and eye shade
- ❏ Binoculars in hard case
- ❏ Roll of transparent tape

- ❏ Adapter — but see if you can eliminate any need for it
- ❏ Transistor radio with extra batteries, or small cassette player
- ❏ Musical instruments — always a hit when you travel

When Traveling with Infants or Toddlers

- ❏ Car seat with cloth liner
- ❏ Disposable diapers
- ❏ Moist foil-wrapped towelettes
- ❏ Cloth diaper or two for changing pad
- ❏ Garbage bags
- ❏ Diaper rash ointment
- ❏ Small packets of tissues
- ❏ Nightlight
- ❏ Flashlights
- ❏ Extra juice
- ❏ Child's cup with drinking spout or collapsible cup
- ❏ Fork and spoon
- ❏ Drinking straws
- ❏ Familiars food — cereal, crackers, noodles
- ❏ Finger foods — cubes of cheese, vegetable sticks
- ❏ Vitamins or fluoride drops
- ❏ Bibs
- ❏ Small toys — figures, cars or trucks, stacking cups, colored pencils, pad of paper
- ❏ Favorite animal or doll
- ❏ Pacifier
- ❏ Compass
- ❏ Transparent tape
- ❏ Insect repellent
- ❏ Baby shampoo and soap
- ❏ Favorite books

ⅢⅡ BUSINESS TRAVEL CHECKLIST ⅢⅡ

Airline	Flight No.	Ticket No.	Cost	Date	Departs City/Time	Arrives City/Time

Name of clerk _____

Date & time of reservation _____ Confirmed? _____

CAR RENTAL

Pick up car where? _____ Discount offered? _____

Shuttle service? _____

Drop off car where? _____

Own insurance policy covers? _____

Cost per day/week $ _____
Insurance $ _____
Mileage charge $ _____
Other charges $ _____
Drop-off fee $ _____
TOTAL $ _____

HOTELS

Name _____

Address _____

Phone No. _____ Cost per day _____

Parking Res. No. _____ Restaurant _____ Recreational Facilities _____

Name _____

Address _____

Phone No. _____ Cost per day _____

Parking Res. No. _____ Restaurant _____ Recreational Facilities _____

USEFUL ADDRESSES

To locate a particular agency, organization, company, product, or publication, look under the major headings listed below. Mailing addresses, telephone and fax numbers, and on-line listings are as current as possible at the time of publication for this section.

HEALTH

Emergency Help

Overseas Citizens' Emergency
 Center
2201 C Street NW
Washington, DC 20520
202-647-5225

Lists of English-Speaking Doctors

International Association for
 Medical Assistance to Travelers
417 Center Street
Lewiston, NY 14092
716-754-4883
Free. Members receive a directory of
English-speaking physicians in 125
countries who will provide twenty-
four-hour care at reasonable fees.
Membership also includes a world
immunization chart and world disease charts, such as a world malaria
risk chart and protection guide. With
a donation, you may receive a world
climate chart that lists seasonal
clothing required and sanitary conditions of milk, water, and food. Also
available for sale is a portable mosquito net.

Emergency Assistance Companies

American Express Global Assist
 Service
United States: 800-554-AMEX
Abroad (call collect): 202-783-7474
Provides emergency assistance to
cardmembers if more than one

hundred miles from home. The hot
line will refer you to a nearby legal or
medical professional, will arrange for
a translator, and will notify your
home or office.

Assist-Card
1001 South Bayshore Drive
Suite 2302
Miami, FL 33131
800-874-2223

Hoteldocs
800-468-3537
Sends an American Medical
Association recruited doctor to your
U.S. hotel room within forty minutes
of your call, at any time of day.

International SOS Assistance, Inc.
P.O. Box 11568
Philadelphia, PA 19116
215-244-1500
Provides emergency assistance to
members. If medical attention cannot
be rendered locally, the traveler will
be evacuated to a place with medical
facilities.

Travel Guard International
1100 Center Point Drive
Stevens Point, WI 54481
Obtain information on this service,
underwritten by the Insurance
Company of North America, through
your travel agent. Offers a 24-hour
emergency claims service, emergency
assistance, medical expenses, baggage and travel documents coverage,
trip cancellation insurance.

Health Aids and Information

International Travelers' Hotline of
  the Centers for Disease Control
404-332-4559
Provides all necessary immunization
information for travelers.

Lifeguard Corporation
Box 15099
Charlotte, NC 28211
800-438-9111
Car decals and iron-on labels alerting
emergency personnel to special conditions, such as allergies or chronic
illnesses.

Medic Alert Foundation
P.O. Box 1009
Turlock, CA 95381
209-668-3333
Fax: 209-669-2450
Provides special bracelets and neck-
laces with emergency information
engraved on them.

PASSPORT AGENCIES

National Passport Center
31 Rochester Avenue
Portsmouth, NH 03801-2900

Boston Passport Agency
Thomas P. O'Neill Federal
  Building, Suite 247
10 Causeway Street
Boston, MA 02202-1094

Chicago Passport Agency
Suite 380
Kluczynski Federal Building
230 South Dearborn Street
Chicago, IL 60604-1564

Honolulu Passport Agency
First Hawaiian Tower
1132 Bishop Street, Suite 500
Honolulu, HI 96813-2809

Houston Passport Agency
Mickey Leland Federal Building
1919 Smith Street
Houston, TX 77002-8049

Los Angeles Passport Agency
Room 13100
11000 Wilshire Boulevard
Los Angeles, CA 90024-3615

Miami Passport Agency
Claude Pepper Federal Office
  Building
51 S.W. First Avenue
Miami, FL 33130-1680

New Orleans Passport Agency
12005 Postal Services Building
701 Loyola Avenue
New Orleans, LA 70113-1931

New York Passport Agency
Room 270
Rockefeller Center
630 Fifth Avenue
New York, NY 10111

Philadelphia Passport Agency
U.S. Customs House, Room 103
200 Chestnut Street
Philadelphia, PA 19106-2970

San Francisco Passport Agency
95 Hawthorne Street, 5th Floor
San Francisco, CA 94102

Seattle Passport Agency
Henry Jackson Federal Building
915 Second Avenue
Seattle, WA 98174

Stamford Passport Agency
One Landmark Square
Broad and Atlantic Streets
Stamford, CT 06901

Washington Passport Agency
1111 19th Street, NW
Washington, DC 20522-1705

Canadian Passport Office
Ottawa, ONT K1A 0G3
A Canadian passport costs $21 and
must be renewed every five years.
Obtain a form (Form A for adults,
Form B for children) at any post
office or travel agency. Call
800-567-9615 for information.

PASSPORT
AND VISA SERVICE

Passport Plus
677 5th Avenue, 5th Floor
New York, NY 10022
800-367-1818
212-759-5540

DISCOUNT
TRAVEL SERVICES

Council Charter
205 E. 42nd Street, 16th Floor
New York, NY 10017
212-661-0311
800-223-7402
800-800-8222
Purchases seats on commercial
airlines flying between Europe
and New York, Boston,
Washington, D.C., Los Angeles,
and San Francisco.

Hotel Reservations Network
800-964-6835
Offers discount hotel reservations in
major U.S. cities.

IBC Pacific, Inc.
Courier Department
1595 El Segundo Boulevard
El Segundo, CA 90245
310-607-0125
Fax: 310-607-0126
E-mail: courierdept@ibcinc.com
Uses couriers on flights between Los
Angeles or San Francisco and seven
cities in Asia: Bangkok, Hong Kong,
Manila, Seoul, Singapore, Taipei, and
Tokyo.

International Association of Air
    Travel Couriers
407-582-8320

Traveler's Advantage
Support Services
3033 South Parker Road
Suite 1000
Aurora, CO 80014
800-255-0200
Discounts on airline, train, and
hotel tickets and tour packages for
domestic and international travel.

Travelocity
E-mail: www.travelocity.com
Offers information on all aspects
of travel.

Worldwide Discount Travel
   Club
1674 Meridian Avenue
Suite 304
Miami Beach, FL 33139

TRANSPORTATION PASSES

Eurailpass
666 Fifth Avenue
6th Floor
New York, NY 10103
212-397-2667

Forsyth Travel Library
9154 West 57th Street
P.O. Box 2975
Shawnee Mission, KS 66201-1375
800-FORSYTH

TRANSPORTATION

Amtrak
800-USA-RAIL
Amtrack offers attractive family
packages, comfortable trains, and
scenic routes.

Caribbean Yacht Company
800-225-2520
Call for information on chartering a
sailboat in St. Thomas.

Europabus Tours
770 Lexington Avenue
New York, NY 10021
212-751-4200

Europe by Car
New York:
1 Rockefeller Plaza
New York, NY 10020
212-581-3040
Fax: 212-246-1458
Internet: www.europebycar.com
California:
9000 Sunset Boulevard
Los Angeles, CA 90069
213-272-0424

French Experience
171 Madison Avenue
New York, NY 10016
212-683-2445
Write for information on renting
canal boats.

Greyhound Bus Lines
800-231-2222

Moorings
800-535-7289
Call for information about chartering
a sailboat in the Caribbean. Six base
locations available.

Nautor's Swan
800-356-7926
Call for information about chartering
a sailboat in St. Martin.

USEFUL ORGANIZATIONS

Amerian Association of Retired
  Persons (AARP)
1919 K Street NW
Washington, DC 20049

AARP Travel Service
5855 Green Valley Circle
Culver City, CA 90230
800-227-7737

American Youth Hostels
P.O. Box 37613
Washington, DC 20013-7613
202-783-6161
Several categories of membership —
Senior (ages 18–59); Senior citizen
(60 and over); Junior (17 and under);
Three-year (ages 18–59); Family
membership (married couples or parents with children); Life membership
(no age limit). With membership you

receive a directory of U.S. hostels,
quarterly magazine, and discounts on
guide books and rail passes. The
International Youth Hostel Handbook
in two volumes covers sixty-four
countries with five thousand hostels.
Volume 1 covers Europe and the
Mediterranean; Volume 2 covers
everywhere else.

At Home Abroad, Inc.
Sutton Town House
405 E. 56th Street, 6-H
New York, NY 10022
212-421-9165
Fax: 212-752-1591
Internet: member.aol.com/
  athomabroad
Offers vacation rentals, specializing in
villas in Tuscany, Provence, Umbria,
and the Caribbean.

Aviation Consumer Action Project
202-638-4000
Founded by Ralph Nader, this organi-
zation publishes a brochure entitled
*Facts and Advice for Airline
Passengers.*

Canadian Hosteling Association
  National Office
33 River Road
Vanier (Ottawa), ONT K1L 8H9
613-237-7884
Call for addresses of regional offices.

Council on International
  Educational Exchange (CIEE)
205 E. 42nd Street
New York, NY 10017
212-661-1414
Write for International Student
Identity Card (also available at CIEE
offices in Boston, Seattle, San
Francisco, Berkeley, Los Angeles, and
San Diego). There is no age limit for
this card, but you must be a full-time
high school or college student. CIEE
also operates low-cost charter flights.

Elderhostel, Inc.
75 Federal Street
Boston, MA 02110-1941
617-426-7788
If you're fifty-five or over (or accompanying your spouse of that age),
you can study for one to four weeks
at colleges and universities around
the country and around the world.
Write and ask for a free catalog, or
look for it in your public library.

Federal Aviation Administration
Consumer Hotline:
  800-322-7873 to report
  consumer complaints

Safety Hotline:
  800-255-1111 to report safety
  violations

Flying Wheels Travel
P.O. Box 382
Owatonna, MN 55060
800-535-6790
Travel agency that specializes in book-
ing tours for the disabled traveler.

International Airline Passengers
  Association
214-404-9980
As a member you can buy travel
accident insurance.

Mobility International USA
P.O. Box 10767
Eugene, OR 97440
541-343-1284
Fax: 541-343-6812
E-mail: miusa@igc.apc.org
Publishes *Over the Rainbow,* a quar-
terly newsletter on travel and interna-
tional educational exchanges for dis-
abled persons, and a book, *A World
of Options: A Guide to International
Educational Exchanges, Community
Service, and Travel for Persons with
Disabilities.*

National Retired Teachers
  Association
1909 K Street NW
Washington, DC 20049
202-872-4700
Membership costs $5 a year.

Rehabilitation International —
  U.S.A.
20 West 40th Street
New York, NY 10018
Publishes a directory of access
guides.

Single World
444 Madison Avenue
New York, NY 10022
This firm offers travel accommodations for people traveling alone.

TransNet
P.O. Box 69
Malverne, NY 11565-0069
516-568-2715
An information clearinghouse and
networking resource for disabled
travelers, covering both domestic
and international travel.

Travel Companion Exchange
Box 833
Amityville, NY 11701
A personalized service that carefully
matches travel companions of all
ages (eighteen to eighty-plus) and
interests.

Travel With Your Children
  (TWYCH)
40 Fifth Avenue
New York, NY 10011
212-477-5524
A resource and information center for
parents and travel agents planning
family travel. Publishes a quarterly
newsletter, *Family Travel Times,* as
well as individual travel sheets and
useful guides covering specific types of
family vacations — nature, adventure,
cruise, sports, learning, and more.

WOMEN'S TRAVEL ORGANIZATIONS

Earthwise Journeys
P.O. Box 42584
Portland, OR 97242
800-344-5309
E-mail: www.teleport.com/
  earthwyz

International Federation of
  Women's Travel Organizations
7432 Caminito Carlotta
San Diego, CA 92120
Write for their handy pamphlet on
tipping customs in foreign countries.

Wild Women Adventures
107 N. Main Street
Sebastopol, CA 05472
707-829-3670
800-992-1322
E-mail: travel@wildwomenadv.com

Womanpower Enterprises
2551 Sumac Circle
St. Paul, MN 55110
800-879-1696
Fax: 612-773-8418
E-mail: estaus@m.com
Focuses on travel to and within Kenya.

NATIONAL TOURISM OFFICES

Antigua Department of Tourism
610 Fifth Avenue
New York, NY 10020
212-541-4117

Aruba Tourist Authority
1000 Harbor Boulevard
Weehawken, NJ 07087
800-862-7822 (800-TO ARUBA)

Australian Tourist Commission
100 Park Avenue
New York, NY 10003
310-229-4870
847-296-4900 (travel planning
  assistance)

Austrian National Tourist Office
500 Fifth Avenue
New York, NY 10110
212-944-6880

Bahamas Tourist Office
150 E. 52nd Street
New York, NY 10022
212-758-2777

Barbados Tourist Board
800 Second Avenue
New York, NY 10017
212-986-6516
800-221-9831

Bermuda Department of Tourism
310 Madison Avenue, Room 201
New York, NY 10017
212-818-9800
800-223-6106

Brazilian Tourism Board
16 W. 46th Street
New York, NY 10036
212-840-3733
212-764-6161

British Tourist Authority
(England, Scotland, Wales,
Northern Ireland)
551 5th Avenue
New York, NY 10022
212-986-2266

Bulgaria Travel Information
Center
41 E. 42nd Street
New York, NY 10017
212-573-5530

Caribbean Tourism Organization
20 East 46th Street
New York, NY 10017
212-682-0435

Cayman Island Department of
Tourism
420 Lexington Avenue
New York, NY 10170
212-682-5582

Colombian Consulate General
10 E. 46th Street
New York, NY 10017
212-949-9898

Costa Rica Permanent Mission to
the United Nations
211 E. 43rd Street
New York, NY 10117
212-986-6373

Curaçao Tourist Board
475 Park Avenue South
New York, NY 10017
212-683-7660

Ecuador National Tourist Office
50 E. 40th Street
New York, NY 10003
212-684-3060

Egyptian Tourist Authority
630 Fifth Avenue
New York, NY 10111
212-332-2570

European Travel Commission
630 Fifth Avenue, Suite 610
New York, NY 10111
212-307-1200

French Government Tourist Office
444 Madison Avenue
New York, NY 10017
212-838-7800

French West Indies
610 Fifth Avenue
New York, NY 10020
212-757-1125

Greek National Tourist
   Organization
645 Fifth Avenue
New York, NY 10022
212-412-5777

Haitian Consulate
271 Madison Avenue
New York, NY 10016
212-697-9767

Hong Kong Tourist Association
590 Fifth Avenue
New York, NY 10036
212-869-5008

Hungarian Tourist Board
150 E. 58th Street
New York, NY 10155
212-355-0240

India Government Tourist Office
30 Rockefeller Plaza
New York, NY 10112
212-586-4901

Indonesia Information Office
5 East 68th Street
New York, NY 10021
212-879-0600

Irish Tourist Board
345 Park Avenue
New York, NY 10154
212-418-0800
800-223-6470

Israel Government Tourist Office
800 Second Avenue
New York, NY 10118
212-560-0650

Italian Government Travel Office
630 Fifth Avenue
Rockefeller Center, Room 1565
New York, NY 10111
212-455-4822 or 4825

Jamaica Tourist Board
801 2nd Avenue
New York, NY 10017
212-856-9727
800-223-5225

Japan National Tourist
   Information
1 Rockefeller Plaza
New York, NY 10111
212-757-5640

Kenya Tourist Office
424 Madison Avenue
New York, NY 10017
212-486-1300

Korea Tourist Office
2 Executive Drive, Suite 750
Fort Lee, NJ 07024
800-868-7567

Mexican Government Tourism
   Office
405 Park Avenue, Room 1002
New York, NY 10022
212-838-2949

Netherlands National Tourist
   Office
355 Lexington Avenue, 21st Floor
New York, NY 10017
212-370-7360

New Zealand Tourist Board
501 Santa Monica Boulevard,
   Suite 300
Santa Monica, CA 90401
800-388-5494
Fax: 310-395-5453

Norwegian Consulate
825 3rd Avenue, 38th Floor
New York, NY 10022
212-421-7333

Philippine Tourism
556 Fifth Avenue
New York, NY 10036
212-575-7915

Puerto Rico Tourism Company
575 Fifth Avenue
New York, NY 10022
212-599-6262
800-223-6530

Quebec Government House
1 Rockefeller Center
New York, NY 10111
212-459-2710
800-363-7777

Romanian National Tourist Office
342 Madison Avenue
New York, NY 10016
212-697-6971

Russian National Tourist Office
800 Third Avenue
New York, NY 10011
212-758-1162

The Tourist Office of Spain
666 Fifth Avenue
New York, NY 10103
212-265-8822

Sri Lanka Board of Tourism
Embassy of Sri Lanka
2148 Wyoming Avenue NW
Washington, DC 20008
202-483-4025

Swiss National Tourist Office
608 Fifth Avenue
New York, NY 10020
212-757-5944

Tahiti Tourist Development Board
444 Madison Avenue
New York, NY 10017
212-838-8663

Taiwan Visitors Association
One World Trade Center, Suite 8855
New York, NY 10048
212-466-0691

Thailand Tourist Office
5 World Trade Center, Suite 2449
New York, NY 10048
212-432-0433

Trinidad and Tobago Tourist
Information
420 Lexington Avenue
New York, NY 10017
212-682-7399
800-232-0082

Turkish Government Tourism
and Information Office
821 United Nations Plaza
New York, NY 10017
212-687-2194

U.S. Department of Commerce
United States Travel and Tourism
Room 1524
14th and Constitution Avenue NW
Washington, DC 20230
202-377-3811 or 2000

Venezuela Tourist Office
7 East 51st Street
New York, NY 10022
212-826-1660

CUSTOMS

U.S. Customs Service
1301 Constitution Avenue NW
Washington, DC 20229-0001
202-622-2000
Distributes **Know Before You Go,** a
useful booklet on customs rules and
regulations, and GSP *and the
International Traveler,* which
discusses duty exemptions for
certain goods under the Generalized
System of Preferences.

GOVERNMENT PUBLICATIONS ON TRAVEL

*Travelers' Tips on Bringing Food,
Plant and Animal Products into
the United States* is available
from the U.S. Department of
Agriculture, Washington, D.C.
20250.

Travel Tips for Mature Citizens
(Pub. No. 8970) is distributed by
the U.S. Government Printing
Office, Washington, DC 20402
(202-783-5238).

The following booklets may be
ordered from the Consumer
Information Center, Pueblo,
CO, 81009 (719-948-3334):

*Access Travel: A Guide to
Accessibility of Airport
Terminals*

Fly Rights 124D
How to get the best fares and how to
cope with problems.

Foreign Entry Requirements 363D
Visa requirements of foreign
countries.

*Lesser Known Areas of the
National Park System* 125D
Listing by state of more than one
hundred seventy national parks.

National Park System Map and Guide 126D
Revised full-color map covers more than three hundred parks, along with activities.

New Horizons for the Air Traveler with a Disability 601D

OTHER PUBLICATIONS

101 Tips for the Mature Traveler
Grand Circle Travel
347 Congress Street, Suite 3A
Boston, MA 02210
617-350-7500
800-221-2610

Jax Fax
Jet Air Transport Exchange, Inc.
397 Post Road
Darien, CT 06820-1413
203-655-8746
A monthly newsletter listing discounted airline seats.

USEFUL PRODUCTS

AM Data Service
67 S. Bedford Street
Burlington, MA 01803
617-229-5853
Carries a pocket guide with diagrams of over seventy-five U.S. airports, showing locations of ticket counters, gates, baggage claims, and car rental agencies.

American Red Cross Automobile First-Aid Kit
Box D
Haworth, NJ 07641
Kit includes bandages and sterile wipes, a waterproof blanket, and scissors.

Caswell-Massey
Mail Order Division
111 Eighth Avenue
New York, NY 10011

The Orvis Company
Route 7A
Manchester, VT 05254-0798
802-362-3622
800-541-3541
Carries many useful travel products, including top-of-the-line, field-tested rolling luggage, travel alarm clocks, packable raincoats and travel vests, money belts, and neck pillows. Company stores are located in a number of cities in the United States and England.

Translator 8000
Langenscheidt Publishers
Maspeth, NY
718-784-0055
Electronic dictionary for French, Spanish, or German. Company also has excellent maps, foreign language dictionaries, and, on CD-ROM, German instructional materials.

Traveler's Checklist
335 Cornwall Bridge Road
Sharon, CT 06069
860-364-0144
Fax: 860-364-0369
Send a dollar to receive this catalog.
Includes money belt, a handheld
|computer called the Road Whiz
Ultra 60,000, a money exchanger/
calculator, smoke/burglar alarm,
adapters, etc.

STATE TOURISM BUREAUS

Alabama Tourism and Travel
401 Adams Avenue
Montgomery, AL 36104
800-252-2262 (800-ALABAMA)

Alaska Office of Tourism
P.O. Box 110801
Juneau, AK 99811
907-465-2010

Arizona Office of Tourism
2702 N. Third Street
Suite 4015
Phoenix, AZ 85004
602-248-1480

Arkansas Department of Parks
and Tourism
1 Capitol Mall
Little Rock, AR 72201
501-682-7777
800-NATURAL

California Division of Tourism
P.O. Box 1499
Sacramento, CA 95812-1499
916-322-1396
800-862-2543

Colorado Travel and Tourism
707 17th Street, Suite 3500
Denver, CO 80202
303-296-3384
800-265-6723 (800-COLORADO)

Connecticut Tourism
865 Brook Street
Rocky Hill, CT 06067
860-258-4355
800-282-6863

Delaware State Chamber of
Commerce
1201 N. Orange, Suite 200
Wilmington, DE 19899
302-655-7221
800-292-9507 (in state)

Washington D.C. Convention and
Visitors Association
1212 New York Avenue NW
Washington, DC 20064
202-789-7000

Florida Division of Tourism
107 W. Gaine Street
Tallahassee, FL 32399
904-487-1462

Georgia Department of Industry,
Trade, and Tourism
Box 1776
Atlanta, GA 30301
404-656-3545

Hawaii Visitors and Convention
Bureau
2270 Kalakaua Avenue
Suite 801
Honolulu, HI 96815
808-923-1811
800-GOHAWAII

Idaho Division of Tourism
Hall of Mirrors
700 West State Street
Boise, ID 83720-0093
208-334-2470
800-635-7820

Illinois Tourism Bureau
James R. Thompson Building
100 W. Randolph, Suite 3-400
Chicago, IL 60601
800-2CONNECT

Indiana Tourism
1 N. Capitol, Suite 700
Indianapolis, IN 46204
317-232-8860

Iowa Tourism
200 E. Grand Avenue
Des Moines, IA 50309
515-281-3100

Kansas Department of
Commerce
700 Southwest Harrison Street
Suite 1300
Topeka, KS 66603
913-296-3481

Kentucky Travel
Capital Plaza Tower, 22nd Floor
500 Mero Street
Frankfort, KY 40601
502-564-4930
800-225-8747

Louisiana Office of Tourism
P.O. Box 94291
Baton Rouge, LA 70804
504-342-8119
800-99GUMBO

Maine Department of Economic
and Commercial Development
59 State House Station
Augusta, ME 04333
207-289-2423

Maryland Office of Tourist
Information
217 E. Redwood Street, 9th Floor
Baltimore, MD 21202
410-767-3400
800-543-1036 (for travel kits)

Massachusetts Office of Tourism
Office of Travel and Tourism
100 Cambridge Street
Boston, MA 02202
617-727-3201
800-227-6277

Michigan Travel Bureau
P.O. Box 30226
Lansing, MI 48909
517-373-0670
800-543-2937

Minnesota Office of Tourism
100 Metro Square
121 7th Place East
St. Paul, MN 55101-2112
612-296-5029
800-657-3700

Mississippi Department of
 Economic Development
Division of Tourism
P.O. Box 1705
Ocean Springs, MS 39566-1705
601-359-3297
800-927-6378

Missouri Division of Tourism
P.O. Box 1055
Jefferson City, MO 65102
573-751-4133
800-877-1234

Travel Montana
1424 Ninth Avenue
Helena, MT 59620
406-444-2654
800-VISITMT (out of state)

Nebraska Division of Travel
 and Tourism
Department of Economic
 Development
301 Centennial Mall South
P.O. Box 94666
Lincoln, NE 68509
402-471-3796
800-228-4307

Nevada Commission on Tourism
Capitol Complex
5151 South Carson Street
Carson City, NV 89710
702-687-4322
800-NEVADA8

New Hampshire Office of Travel
 and Tourism
P.O. Box 1856
Concord, NH 03302
603-271-2343
800-FUNINNH

New Jersey Division of Travel
 and Tourism
1 West State, CN 826
Trenton, NJ 08625
609-292-2470
800-JERSEY7

New Mexico Department of
 Tourism
491 Old Santa Fe Trail
Santa Fe, NM 87503
505-827-7400
800-545-2040

New York State Division of Tourism
1515 Broadway
Albany, NY 12245
518-827-6255
800-225-5697

North Carolina Travel and
 Tourism Division
301 N. Wilmington Street
Raleigh, NC 27601
919-733-4171
800-847-4862

North Dakota Tourism
604 E. Boulevard Avenue
Bismarck, ND 58505
701-328-2525
800-435-5663

Ohio Travel and Tourism
P.O. Box 1001
Columbus, OH 43216
614-466-8844
800-848-1300

Oklahoma Tourism and
  Recreation Department
P.O. Box 52002
Oklahoma City, OK 73152
405-521-2464
800-652-6552

Oregon Tourism
775 Summer Street NE
Salem, OR 97310
503-986-0000
800-547-7842

Pennsylvania Travel Bureau
456 Forum Building
Harrisburg, PA 17120
717-787-5453
800-VISITPA

Rhode Island State Office of
  Tourism
Economic Development
  Corporation
1 W. Exchange Street
Providence, RI 02903
401-277-2601
800-556-2484

South Carolina Division of
  Tourism
Box 71
Columbia, SC 29202
803-734-0135
800-553-7752

South Dakota Division of
  Tourism
Capital Lake Plaza
711 E. Wells Avenue
Pierre, SD 57501
605-773-3301
800-952-3625

Tennessee Tourist Development
P.O. Box 23170
Nashville, TN 37203
615-741-2158

Texas Department of
  Transportation
Travel Division
P.O. Box 5064
Austin, TX 78763-5064

CCVC: Texas Travel Information
  Center
c/o Mary Jackson
112 E. 11th Street
Austin, TX 78701
512-463-8586
800-452-9292

Utah Travel Council
Council Hall, Capitol Hill
Salt Lake City, UT 84114
801-538-1030
800-200-1160

Vermont Travel Division
134 State Street
Montpelier, VT 05601-1471
802-828-3236
800-VERMONT

Virginia Division of Tourism
901 E. Byrd Street
Richmond, VA 23219
804-786-4484
800-VISITVA

Washington State Tourism
101 General Administration
  Building
P.O. Box 42500
Olympia, WA 98504-2500
360-753-5600
800-544-1800 (for travel kits)

West Virginia Tourism
2101 Washington Street E
Charleston, WV 25305
304-558-2286
800-225-5982

Wisconsin Tourism
P.O. Box 7606
Madison, WI 53707-7606
608-266-2161
800-432-8747

Wyoming Tourism
Frank Norris, Jr., Travel Center
Cheyenne, WY 82002
307-777-7777
800-225-5996

FREIGHTERS

Discount Travel International
  Club
7563 Haverford Avenue
Philadelphia, PA 19151
215-925-6172

Freighter World Cruises
180 South Lake Avenue, Suite 335
Pasadena, CA 91101
818-449-3106
A new and updated edition of
their *Freighter Space Advisory*
publication is available twice a
month. Write to ask for the cost of
the guide.

Trav-L-Tips, Freighter Travel
  Association
163-09 Depot Road
Flushing, NY 11358
718-939-2400
Write or call for listings of freighter
routes, departure dates, and costs.

The most common shipping
lines in freighter travel are
Polish Ocean Lines, Prudential
Lines, Lykes Brothers, and
American President Lines.
Ask your travel agent for
addresses and phone numbers
of these organizations.

FOREIGN VACATION RENTALS

At Home Abroad
405 East 56th Street
New York, NY 10022
212-421-9165

Villas and Apartments Abroad
420 Madison Avenue
New York, NY 10017
212-759-1025
Listings include the Caribbean,
Mexico, Costa Rica, Italy, France,
and England.

ONLINE SERVICES

Online travel-related services
change frequently. New ones are
added all the time, and addresses
sometimes change.

Internet Travel Network
http://www.itn.net

Microsoft Expedia
http://www.expedia.msn.com

PC Travel
http://www.pctravel.com

Reservations.com
http://www.reservations.com

Travelocity
http://www.travelocity.com

TravelWeb
http://www.travelweb.com

INDEX

Note: Page references in *italics* refer to illustrations.